A Citizens Legal Manual

Do-it-Yourself Law

HALT's Guide to Self-Help
Books, Kits & Software

**James C. Turner
Theresa Meehan Rudy
Edward J. Tannouse**

ISBN 0-910073-24-4

Also by HALT:
Using a Lawyer
The Legal Resource Directory
If You Want to Sue a Lawyer
Your Guide to Living Trusts & Other Trusts
Wills
Real Estate
Everyday Contracts
Small Claims Court
The Smart Consumer
Using the Law Library
Legal Rights for Seniors
The Easy Way to Probate
You, Your Family and the Law

Graphic Design and Production: Cheryl Matcho
Proofreading: Katherine Wertheim

ACKNOWLEDGMENTS

We would like to gratefully express our appreciation to the following individuals and organizations for their support in making this book possible:

The Ruth Eleanor Bamberger and John Ernst Bamberger Memorial Fund, David Bell, Katherine S. Broderick, Louis Clark, the Compton Foundation, Consumer Federation of America, CQ Productions, Beth M. Daley, Edward Dempsey, the Everett Philanthropic Fund, the Fund for Constitutional Government, the Government Accountability Project, Paul J. Haussman, James H. Johnston, the T. James Kavanaugh Foundation, Jennifer Keller, Herman Max Leibowitz, Jon S. Legallet, Tom W. Lyons, Conrad Martin, Lloyd McAulay, George A. Miller, the Stewart R. Mott Charitable Trust, Beatrice Moulton, Andrew Joseph Rudy, Anita Stafford, the Stern Family Fund, Marquita Sykes, Eric Thorson, Beatrice M. Thompson, Robert S. Tigner, Margery Austin Turner, Keith Wentz, May Yoneyama, and all the publishers who submitted material for review.

But most of all, we are grateful to the 50,000 citizens whose support and commitment to HALT—*An Organization of Americans for Legal Reform* makes it possible to do work like this.

JCT, TMR, and EJT
January, 1999

TABLE OF
CONTENTS

CHAPTER 6: Estate Planning   127

CHAPTER 7: Small Business   185

DO-IT-YOURSELF LAW

Beyond Cookie-Cutter Form Books
and Boilerplate One-Size-Fits-All Documents

All of us can expect to face many legal issues during our lives. Almost everything we do—attending a school, renting an apartment, getting married, becoming parents, getting divorced, even dying—is governed by law.

Understanding the law can help you protect your rights. The products reviewed in this book will not only help you understand your legal rights in a variety of situations, they'll teach you how to "be your own lawyer" for most common tasks.

Despite the ominous warning that "a man who represents himself has a fool for a client," today tens of millions of Americans are taking advantage of do-it-yourself law books, software, and kits. When it was founded 20 years ago, HALT was one of the pioneers in publishing self-help law books. Over the past decade, there has been a literal explosion in the number of high-quality products that let Americans take charge of their own legal affairs.

With so many products available, what is the right choice for your legal needs? That is the question this book tries to answer.

Your need for help in dealing with the legal system depends on the complexity of the legal issues involved, your own education and experience, and the time and energy you are willing to invest to deal with matters on your own.

Most legal tasks that confront ordinary people—such as writing a simple will, filing for an uncontested divorce, creating a simple living trust, changing your name, correcting a charge card error, filing suit in a small claims court, becoming an organ donor, filing an income tax return or probating a small estate— are really "cookie-cutter" jobs that call for minimal expertise. Most people can quickly and competently complete these routine tasks with the help of do-it-yourself law books or software.

But consumers can also use these products to help with more complex legal tasks—such as disputes that involve large sums of money or ones that are contested by others who have hired lawyers. Do-it-yourself products will help you understand and control your own legal affairs if you have to hire a paralegal or a lawyer, and will save you money because you can do part of the work yourself.

UNMET LEGAL NEEDS

The self-help law movement grows—over the strident objections of the legal establishment—because lawyers have priced themselves out of the reach of most ordinary Americans. Face it, lawyers are expensive. Many people simply cannot afford to pay hundreds or thousands of dollars to deal with their routine legal needs.

A comprehensive nationwide study conducted for the American Bar Association in the mid-1990s found that 71 percent of low-income and 61 percent of moderate-income households cannot afford to deal with lawyers or the court system when they have legal problems. Instead, many handled problems on their own, or sought help from somebody other than a lawyer, for example an accountant, an independent paralegal or a realtor. Today, in Arizona, Florida and California, the percentage of people filing "*pro se*" (without a lawyer) in domestic and bankruptcy cases far exceeds those represented by lawyers.

Some courthouses and local bar associations are responding to the needs of *pro se* litigants by distributing court-approved fill-in-the-blank legal forms or installing automated kiosk machines that help people complete their own legal paper-work. But by and large, the legal profession has not been as accommodating to the masses who want to create their own wills and trusts, buy or sell property, or open a business without hiring a lawyer. In fact the opposite is true.

SELF-HELP AND THE UNAUTHORIZED PRACTICE OF LAW

Attacks on the legal self-help movement by the organized bar have increased in recent years despite the fact that millions of Americans want to do much of their own legal work and cannot afford to pay a lawyer to do it.

As this book goes to press, at least three of the most prominent do-it-yourself legal publishers—Nolo Press, Parsons Technology and Block Financial—are either being investigated or prosecuted for the "unauthorized practice of law." Their crime? Distributing products that allow people to complete their own wills, trusts and other legal documents without the assistance of a lawyer.

Over the years, the legal establishment has shown amazing tenacity in attacking and often crushing its competition—whether from lawyers who attended "unaccredited" law schools, paralegals providing legal assistance directly to consumers, or companies that produce self-help legal products.

In 1930, the first American Bar Association Committee to ever deal with unauthorized practice of law issues was formed. Less than a decade later, 400 state and local bar associations had formed similar committees. Since the 1930s hundreds of people and organizations have been hauled before these committees and put out of business.

The threat of being put out of business has intimidated some in the do-it-yourself movement. Prominent, large-print disclaimers can be found in their self-help products, cautioning the reader that "the publisher and author are not engaged in rendering legal, accounting, or other professional services" and that "if legal advice or other expert assistance is required, the services of a competent professional person should be sought."

Despite these disclaimers, state bars are accelerating their prosecutions of nonlawyers and self-help legal publishers who assist consumers in doing their own legal work.

But lawyers are on the losing side of this argument. Technology is rapidly changing the way we communicate, whether lawyers like it or not. Personal computers, CD-ROMs, the Internet and e-mail now govern how much and how quickly information is shared, and entrepreneurs see the writing on the wall. It's only a matter of time before all of us will have access to a variety of interactive legal forms that can be purchased on the Internet with a credit card. The delivery of legal services is changing and, in the end, consumers will be the big winners.

The emergence of new legal products that directly serve consumers at their home computers or over the internet has been dubbed "e-law" by *Legal Times* columnist James H. Johnston, who sees it as offering "exciting opportunities for innovation and enterprise in the legal profession," and as a possible answer to "delivering legal services to the poor." Johnston also predicts that bar associations will not get far with "unauthorized practice of law arguments if e-law proves popular with the consumer. After all, the primary purpose of regulating the practice of law should be to protect consumers, not lawyers." *(Legal Times, November 2, 1998).*

With a growing number of products already available and new technology that will offer consumers even more alternatives, we believe that do-it-yourself legal materials are here to stay. This book is an effort to help you take advantage of these new opportunities to control your own legal affairs.

HOW WE SELECTED THE PRODUCTS REVIEWED

When we decided to write a guide to do-it-yourself legal materials, we asked ourselves two questions:

• What are the most common legal needs people have?
• Which products best address those needs?

To answer the first question, we identified common legal problems people encounter during their lifetimes, and concentrated our searches there. We contacted publishers that produce both self-help and traditional legal materials, and searched for other titles listed on the Internet, Books-in-Print, local library databases, and the Library of Congress. We also contacted traditional legal publishers, such as West Publishing and Commerce Clearing House, but decided against including their publications since most are written in legalese, and are priced for lawyers and law firms.

The selection of national titles reviewed for this book, while thorough, is not exhaustive; it represents the most popular products, and includes the best materials available from the most reputable publishers in the U.S. New products are added to the market monthly, so it is almost impossible to completely canvass all the works in print.

WHAT PRODUCTS ARE INCLUDED?

The products we chose to review cover the most common legal concerns you'll face. Legal encyclopedias or "lawyer-in-a-box" products cover a variety of legal topics under one title. Other products address one specific topic like buying a home, running a business or writing a will.

All legal encyclopedias vary in the topics they cover, but as a rule they include consumer matters, finance and credit, employment issues, purchase and sales agreements, marriage and parenting, separation and divorce, real estate, taxes, estate planning, health care, bankruptcy, and retirement.

Years ago, lawyer-in-a-box products usually offered about 20 legal forms; now some products boast over 300, with most providing 100 to 150. And some CD-ROM products include, in addition to legal forms, an amazing amount of legal information. It's not uncommon, for example, to find two or more legal reference books and a complete law dictionary.

We also reviewed products that cover family law, property issues, tax, bankruptcy, estate planning, and small businesses.

Although there are good products on the market, we did not review self-help materials on incorporating a business or filing for a patent, copyright or trademark, because these topics are not ones that most people deal with during their lives.

All of the products reviewed in this book are written for a national audience. This means they generally produce legal forms and agreements that are legally valid in all 50 states (although Louisiana, with state laws that reflect its history as a French colony, is often omitted). There are also many state-specific titles on the market you may want to consider. Appendix 1 includes the names of publishers that produce state-specific materials.

KINDS OF PRODUCTS

Most do-it-yourself legal products use one of two basic approaches. Some products provide a general library of legal information, standardized forms, and instructions on how to complete them. Other products use interactive computer programs that ask you a series of questions, and then produce completed forms, such as wills, prenuptial agreements and powers of attorney. A few products give you the option of selecting from a library of forms or using an interview process.

The kind of product you decide to use will depend on your specific legal needs, the amount of instruction you require, whether or not you have access to a computer, and the amount of time you can spare to do it yourself.

If you prefer to have most of the work done for you, you might be better off investing in interactive software. The finished product is a personalized legal document, often state-specific, that incorporates the information you have provided through a question and answer interview.

If a legal document is created this way, however, you are not usually allowed to modify its language. What you can do is change your original answers and generate a new legal form that reflects those changes. For example, you can decide to appoint your sister Elizabeth instead of your brother Matthew as executor of your will.

You generally cannot, however, change the document language that describes the powers that can be exercised by the executor of your will. Not being able to edit the legal document is actually a safety precaution—it prevents you from making changes that might get you into legal trouble down the road.

The other type of product offers a template legal form. Books and kits typically include pre-printed fill-in-the-blank documents that can be photocopied and completed. If a computer disk is included, you can easily edit the form's language to fit your particular circumstances, and then generate a professional looking document. The downside, of course, is that in making changes, you could add or delete words that change the meaning of your document, so these products are best suited for careful and committed do-it-yourselfers.

CRITERIA USED TO EVALUATE PRODUCTS

We used a grading system to rate each of the products reviewed in this book. In evaluating do-it-yourself software, we prefer substance over "bells and whistles," so products that provide clear, concise explanations that anyone can understand score higher than those that rely on fancy "talking head" videos of three-piece suited Harvard Law School professors delivering impressive lectures.

Each product was evaluated in six different areas:

Accuracy. Good do-it-yourself products are accurate. Does the product provide correct and up-to-date information on the legal topics it discusses? Are laws provided for all 50 states? Is online help available? Is information provided on how to research current law?

Comprehensiveness. Do-it-yourself books and software should be relatively complete—you shouldn't have to buy

law dictionaries or separate reference books to understand and use a good do-it-yourself product. A product
can be up-to-date, but not very comprehensive. We
looked at the level of detail of the discussion given. Was
it thorough? Were there glaring (or subtle) omissions?
Does the text help you find other legal resources and web
sites? Does it use clear examples to illustrate its points?

Plain Language and Glossary. Good self-help law books and
software provide information and legal forms written in
plain-language that anyone can understand, not legalese.
Glossaries are especially valuable to nonlawyers. It's a
lot easier to look in one place for legal definitions than it
is to search through a whole book for the chapter or
section that discusses a particular concept.

Easy to Use. Do-it-yourself products are not useful unless
they are easy to use. Here we looked at how the material
is presented and the quality of the step-by-step instructions given for completing forms. Is the text well-organized? Are reference charts, worksheets, and checklists
included? Does the book have an index?

Red Flags. You should not have to search for warnings. Are
areas that warrant special attention flagged in any special
way (with special icons, capital letters, or boldface print)?
Does the product clearly tell you when you may need to
consult a professional, or to consult other resources?

Quality of Legal Forms. Do-it-yourself documents should
be acceptable to courts and government agencies. What
does the finished product look like? If pre-printed, fill-
in-the-blank forms are provided, are they legible and
easy to complete? Do computer-generated forms print
well or are there formatting or bad page-break problems
that need to be corrected?

Disclaimer. We've also reprinted the disclaimer statements from each product so you will know what its authors say about their product's or software's limitations.

After we assessed the six areas, we assigned a final grade (from A to F) to each product we reviewed and rated them in four groups–HALT Do-it-Yourself Best Buys, Recommended, Good Value and Not Recommended. This final grade also reflects the product's cost, our assessment of its value, and our judgment about which consumers should use it.

There are some truly extraordinary do-it-yourself products on the market today–such as *WillMaker* from Nolo Press and *TurboTax* from Intuit. These products were easy selections as HALT Do-it-Yourself Best Buys. We have also included many other fine products that will help you take charge of your legal affairs. But we also reviewed some popular products that we cannot recommend; they are included so you will know what to avoid as well as what to buy.

———

Being your own lawyer has never been easier. If you're willing to invest a relatively small amount of money and a fair amount of your time, you can create sound legal documents for most common legal needs. The tools are there, so roll up your sleeves and take charge of this part of your life.

1

LEGAL ENCYCLOPEDIAS
"LAWYER-IN-A-BOX"

Just think of it. Scores of legal forms at your fingertips and the information you need to complete each form for less than $100. Sometimes a lot less. This chapter examines the growing number of "lawyer-in-a-box" software packages and books available today. We look at three basic areas—what's covered, how well it is covered and how easy it is to use.

The good news is that there are quite a few reliable and easy-to-use products on the market. The better news is that many of these products, especially those that include computer software, are improving with each passing year.

The products we reviewed offer a variety of legal forms and agreements on everything from developing an estate plan—complete with will, trust and durable power of attorney—to drafting simple contracts, and handling consumer problems, like debt collection and credit disputes. Some products also cover other areas of law, such as real estate, small claims, and home repair. With most packages, you get a library of 100 or more forms.

Two basic formats exist: Pre-printed boilerplate forms that cannot be customized, and software that allows you to tailor the legal form to your needs.

Today many legal self-help publishers also include a form disk or CD-ROM with their printed materials. The disk includes the printed forms found in the form book or kit, and can be edited as needed.

CD-ROM software for your home computer is usually interactive, allowing you to create a customized legal form after answering a series of questions. In addition, CDs come packed with lots of extra information specific to the document being drafted and related areas of law. Most CDs also include law dictionaries and "talking head" video presentations. Newer versions even flash warnings across the screen if you've omitted important information or filled in information incorrectly.

Three exceptional products stand out: *101 Law Forms for Personal Use* from Nolo Press, *Home Legal Advisor '98* from Kiplinger, and *Quicken Family Lawyer 99 Deluxe* from Parsons. Each is an extraordinary value for do-it-yourself consumers, and is recommended wholeheartedly as HALT Do-it-Yourself Best Buys.

101 Law Forms for Personal Use

1st Edition
by Robin Leonard & Ralph Warner
Nolo Press, Berkeley, California, 1998
304 pages, $24.95
(800) 992-6656

HALT
Do-it-Yourself
Best Buy

In addition to forms that you might expect to find in a legal encyclopedia (for example, contracts to buy and sell real estate or personal property, simple wills, powers of attorney, promissory notes, and releases), ***101 Law Forms for Personal Use*** includes forms that are overlooked in other products, but which are extremely helpful for consumers. These include forms for the care of children, elderly and pets; home repair, maintenance or remodeling; handling personal finances; hiring household help; living together; preparing for divorce or separation; settling legal disputes; and dealing with direct marketers. ***101 Law Forms*** also includes a form disk and index.

Accuracy   **Grade: A**
> ***101 Law Forms*** provides a thorough and plain-language overview of contract law, the Uniform Commercial Code and other laws governing each agreement. The forms are written in plain language and often include optional clauses so readers can customize them.

Comprehensiveness   **Grade: B⁺**
> As mentioned, ***101 Law Forms*** provides many legal forms you will not find anywhere else, such as forms to get rid of telemarketers, pet-care agreements and housekeeping service agreements. But the book leaves out forms consumers routinely want and which can be found in many other publications, such as living trusts, living wills and

durable powers of attorney for health care. That criticism aside, *101 Law Forms* explains what each form does, includes applicable laws and gives helpful hints, such as web sites to visit or worksheets to complete before filling in the form. For example, in Chapter 6 "Buying a House" the authors recommend visiting one or more web sites for information on agents, lender rates and different geographical areas.

The book also comes with a PC (MS-DOS) formatted form disk and can be used by any PC running Windows or DOS. Mac users require PC Exchange software (which is now built into the operating system) to access the forms on the disk.

Plain Language and Glossary   **Grade: A⁻**

Plain language is used in the text and the forms. Although the authors' statement that "contracts in this book are written in everyday (but legal) language," is generally accurate, legal terms are used such as *material breach, assign,* and *encumbrance*. A glossary that defines these and other terms used in the agreements is not included but would be helpful to consumers.

Easy to Use   **Grade: A⁺**

101 Law Forms includes some of the best step-by-step instruction we've seen on actually filling out the forms, including Editing and Adding to the Forms; Describing People, Events and Property; Selecting From Several Choices (among clauses); Preparing, Signing and Storing the Forms; Requiring a Spouse's Signature; and Notaries and Witnesses. There's also valuable information on using alternative dispute resolution clauses.

Red Flags   **Grade: A**

Areas that warrant special attention are flagged with special icons. Readers are told when they may need to contact a lawyer, when other resources should be consulted, whether they can skip or skim a section and more.

Quality of Legal Forms   **Grade: B⁺**

The forms are easily photocopied and completed, or computer generated. The computer-generated forms look more professional, because you can edit out unnecessary language. Form preparers have to be careful, however, not to edit out relevant information, and remember to re-number clauses in the agreement if irrelevant clauses are taken out.

Disclaimer

"We've done our best to give you useful and accurate information in this book. But laws and procedures change frequently and are subject to differing interpretations. If you want legal advice backed by a guarantee, see a lawyer. If you use this book, it's your responsibility to make sure that the facts and general advice contained in it are applicable to your situation."

Overall   **Grade: A**

101 Law Forms provides a great selection of legal and practical forms for personal use at a very reasonable price. The lack of a simple trust, living will or durable power of attorney for health care will bother some consumers who want to find everything they need in one book. Overall, however, ***101 Law Forms*** identifies some of the most common legal needs a consumer will have and provides them easy-to-use forms to meet those needs. At $24.95, ***101 Law Forms*** is an exceptional value that allows virtually any do-it-yourselfer to produce and complete professional-looking legal forms on a home computer that cover a wide variety of common problems.

HALT
Do-it-Yourself
Best Buy

Kiplinger's Home Legal Advisor '98

Deluxe Multimedia Edition 1998
Block Financial Corporation
Kansas City, Missouri, 1998
CD ROM Software for PC and Mac, $29.95
(800) 813-7940

HALT
Do-it-Yourself
Best Buy

Kiplinger's Home Legal Advisor '98 CD-ROM includes three general reference books: the Home Legal Guide, Kiplinger's Handbook of Personal Law and a Law Dictionary. Other advanced features are a "Document Guide" that interviews you about your legal needs and provides a follow-up report; a file of 71 legal documents; a "Party List," which allows you to store important information about yourself and other individuals; a "Help" button that provides on-screen assistance; and an "Exit" button to quickly leave the program.

The Home Legal Guide provides a good overview of the law in ten areas: General Information, Employment Issues, Consumer Matters, Finance and Credit, General Law, Estate Planning, Real Estate, Marriage, Health Care and Travel.

The Handbook of Personal Law provides additional information on twelve areas of law including: Living with the Law, Your Lawyer, The Law and Your Finances, Your Car, Buying and Selling a Home, Your Home and the Law, Your Workplace Rights and Retirement, Your Medical Rights, Marriage and Other Personal Partnerships, Ending a Marriage, Parenthood and Your Estate.

It's obvious that the package was reviewed by lawyers since, even though a do-it-yourself product, consumers are encouraged at almost every turn to work with a knowledgable local attorney.

Accuracy   **Grade: A**
    Home Legal Advisor provides an in-depth and accurate

discussion of all the legal topics covered and the individual forms provided. Recent changes in the law are included, for example tax law changes that affect estate planning through the year 2006.

Comprehensiveness   **Grade: A⁻**

Home Legal Advisor is a comprehensive household resource that provides over 70 different legal forms for personal use. General discussions of the law can be found in two reference books, *The Home Legal Guide* and *The Handbook of Personal Law* and definitions to over 4,000 legal terms are given in the *Law Dictionary*.

Each legal form includes a document discussion or talking-head video. Whether you read or listen, you'll get an excellent overview of "What" the document is, "Why" you would want to use it, and "How" to fill it out. You are alerted to other important information such as whether the form needs to be notarized, recent changes in the law, and whether you need to have it reviewed by a lawyer.

For the more standard legal forms (wills, trusts, powers of attorney), Mac users only have access to boilerplate, fill-in-the-blank versions, not state-specific forms. Because the forms are written for a general audience and attempt to cover every eventuality, a simple will becomes a lengthy document filled with legalese and lots of unnecessary language.

Plain Language and Glossary   **Grade: A⁻**

The legal discussions found in the reference books and under the individual document discussion buttons are written in plain language and are easy to understand. The forms are also usually easy to understand, but a few of them, particularly the estate planning and real estate documents, include legalese that could be avoided. *Home Legal Advisor* includes a comprehensive and impressive law dictionary with search capabilities, but it reads a lot like Black's Law Dictionary (the standard dictionary for

lawyers, judges and law students). For example, it frequently uses legalese to define legal terms, making it less
accessible to the layperson.

Easy to Use   **Grade: A⁺**
Installation is straightforward for both Windows and Mac
users. Once installed, ***Home Legal Advisor*** is easy to
navigate and use. You can flip back and forth to different files through clearly marked buttons and links. The
forms are easy to complete. To select a document, you
double click on its name from the "Create New Document" file. A window immediately pops up that explains
what the different color text in the form means. Red text
indicates a place where you need to make a decision (for
example, filling in the name of your children's guardian).
Green text, if clicked on, provides a fuller plain-language
discussion of the clause and blue text indicates areas you
have already completed. The window also provides step-
by-step instructions on exactly how to complete the form.
You can easily edit the document on screen, save it to a
separate file and then "Open Saved Document" to work
on it later.

Red Flags   **Grade: B**
Home Legal Advisor includes warnings about when state
law varies, when forms should be reviewed by lawyers,
and when additional resources should be consulted, but
you have to go hunting for them. Other software packages now flash warnings across the screen if you're about
to delete important language or goof-up in some other
way.

Quality of Legal Forms   **Grade: A**
Home Legal Advisor allows you to produce great looking documents on a home computer.

Disclaimer

"The user acknowledges that Block Financial Corporation, The Kiplinger Washington Editors, Inc. and Teneron Corporation do not practice law or provide legal advice, are not engaged in rendering legal, accounting or other professional services and are not rendering such professional services with regard to Kiplinger's Home Legal Advisor. The user acknowledges that laws vary from state to state and change over time. The final documents should be reviewed by a lawyer before use. Where a document is to be negotiated with another party, the user should consult an attorney prior to the start of negotiations. Use of Kiplinger's Home Legal Advisor constitutes agreement to the foregoing."

Overall   **Grade: A**

Home Legal Advisor provides a comprehensive household resource for those who have home computers with CD-ROM. It's packed with lots of information in easy-to-understand language. The lack of state-specific forms for Mac users is a drawback, but the boilerplate forms are usable. At $29.95, **Home Legal Advisor** is an exceptional value that allows virtually any do-it-yourselfer to produce complete and professional-looking legal documents that cover a wider variety of common problems.

HALT
Do-it-Yourself
Best Buy

Quicken Family Lawyer 99 Deluxe
Parsons Technology, Hiawatha, Iowa, 1998
CD-ROM software for Windows 3.1/95 and Mac
$39.95
(800) 779-6000

HALT
Do-it-Yourself
Best Buy

Quicken Family Lawyer 99 Deluxe is an integrated software package that includes over 100 legal forms, ranging from contracts, deeds and wills to consumer complaint letters and personal medical instructions. The software interviews you to suggest which document you should create, and includes split-screen step-by-step instructions for completing each form. ***Family Lawyer 99*** includes a 7,000 entry *Plain-Language Law Dictionary*, and the American Bar Association's *Family Legal Guide*, which provides detailed summaries of the legal system, family law, real estate, consumer law and employment. Harvard Law Professor and "Good Morning America" legal editor Arthur Miller serves as ***Family Lawyer 99's*** talking head in brief videos covering common legal concerns. The package also includes separate estate planning software, which provides additional options and information about wills and living trusts.

Accuracy   **Grade: A**
   Family Lawyer 99 offers concise explanations that accurately summarize the law that applies to each form, along with background information in three other areas: Reasons to Create, which helps you decide whether you need to use a particular form; Before You Begin, a list of the information you need to complete the form, and Reasons to Update, which helps you keep your legal documents current. ***Family Lawyer 99*** includes forms for all 50

states and the District of Columbia, and tailors each form to the requirements for the state where you reside. The package also includes links to the Parsons Technology webpages where consumers can download files that will update *Family Lawyer 99* to reflect changes in state law and to add new forms.

Comprehensiveness **Grade: A⁻**

Family Lawyer 99 covers an extremely wide breadth of topics and provides multiple resources to help consumers understand their options. A glaring omission, however, is the failure to provide any information, forms or guidance on personal bankruptcy procedures.

Plain Language and Glossary **Grade: A⁻**

Family Lawyer 99 successfully avoids almost all legalese and uses language that should be accessible to most consumers. It also includes *The Plain-Language Law Dictionary*, an extensive 7,000 entry, searchable database that defines legal terminology. While this resource is impressively thorough, the definitions are sometimes less than helpful to nonlawyers. For example, the legal term *a priori* is defined as follows "To reason *a priori* is to conclude that from what has existed previously, certain effects must necessarily follow (Latin)," and the term "joint and several" is defined as "An expression denoting unity, as distinguished from separate or individual." The ABA Family Legal Guide also includes a separate glossary of legal terms.

Easy to Use **Grade: A**

Family Lawyer 99 uses simple and straightforward interviews to suggest documents for each user, includes step-by-step instructions for filling out forms and uses highlighted text to link users to explanatory materials.

Red Flags   **Grade: B⁺**

Family Lawyer 99 includes many discussions of potential pitfalls, but the product's overall approach is to serve as the expert and select the right forms for you. This means that there is no occasion to discuss the state-by-state differences in the law, which may make some consumers uneasy. The completed, printed forms also include highlighted warnings about what steps must be taken to create a valid document.

Quality of Legal Forms   **Grade: A⁺**

Family Lawyer 99 produces professional-looking documents.

Disclaimers

Multiple disclaimers are included in this product:

Family Lawyer 99 "This program provides forms and information about the law. We cannot and do not provide information about your exact situation. For example, we can provide a form for a lease, along with information on state laws and issues frequently addressed in leases. But we cannot decide that our programs lease is appropriate for you. Because we cannot decide which forms are best for your individual situation, you must use your own judgment and, to the extent you believe appropriate, the assistance of a lawyer."

"**Family Lawyer** is designed to provide information and forms you may find helpful. It is provided to you with the understanding that Parsons Technology is not engaged in providing legal advice or other professional services. It is not intended to replace legal advice and if legal advice or other expert assistance is required, the services of a competent and qualified lawyer or other professional should be sought."

ABA Family Legal Guide "Points of view or opinions in the software of The American Bar Association Family Legal Guide or any product with which the software of The American Bar Association Family Legal Guide might be sold, do not necessarily represent the official policies or positions of the American Bar Association. This product is sold with the understanding that neither the author nor the publisher are engaged in rendering legal service. If legal advice or other expert assistance is required, the services of a competent professional person should be sought. This product is not a substitute for a lawyer, nor does it attempt to answer all questions about all situations you might encounter."

Overall   **Grade: A**

For the do-it-yourself consumer who wants a comprehensive computer-based guide to common legal forms, at $39.95 *Quicken Family Lawyer 99 Deluxe* is an exceptional value that allows virtually any do-it-yourselfer to produce complete and professional-looking legal documents on a home computer with CD-ROM.

HALT
Do-it-Yourself
Best Buy

Legal-Wise: Self-Help Legal Guide for Everyone
3rd Edition
by Carl W. Battle
Allworth Press, New York, New York, 1996
208 pages, $18.95
(800) 491-2808

Recommended

An inexpensive, hard copy (no computer disks) collection of 38 basic legal forms, *Legal-Wise: Self-Help Legal Guide for Everyone* covers hiring a lawyer, writing a will, basic probate procedures, living trusts, living wills, powers of attorney, real estate sales, leases, contracts, divorce, name changes, small claims, releases, consumer transactions, copyrights, trademarks, and bankruptcy. *Legal-Wise* also includes other useful guidance for consumers such as how to make organ donations, protecting your privacy, and how to handle an IRS audit, as well as an appendix listing other sources of legal information.

Accuracy   **Grade: B⁺**

Legal-Wise offers concise explanations that accurately summarize the law that applies to each of the areas it discusses, and the forms it includes accurately apply these general legal principles. State-by-state variations in law are not discussed in detail, but most of the areas covered by *Legal-Wise* are governed by the same general legal principles. Some guidance on where to find state law exemptions for bankruptcy proceedings would be a helpful addition.

Comprehensiveness   **Grade: B**

Legal-Wise covers a wide breadth of topics in a fairly brief publication. While its discussion of each area of law is relatively thorough, many details that may affect consumers are only mentioned in passing. Each area discussed by *Legal-Wise* includes practical, commonsense advice for consumers—a real plus for this concise publication.

Plain Language and Glossary **Grade: B+**
Legal-Wise successfully avoids almost all legalese and uses language that should be accessible to most consumers. It does not include a glossary, although most legal terms are explained in the text. For such a brief publication, the lack of a glossary is a major shortcoming.

Easy to Use **Grade: A**
Legal-Wise includes step-by-step instructions and checklists to help consumers do it themselves.

Red Flags **Grade: C**
Although *Legal-Wise* includes a wealth of practical advice for consumers and tries to alert them to many potential pitfalls, the warnings contained in its legal summaries are not comprehensive. In addition, there are no icons, boldface or other markings to help ensure that the warnings are found by readers.

Quality of Legal Forms **Grade: B+**
Legal-Wise includes 38 basic legal forms that are legible, easy to read and produce high-quality photocopies. The step-by-step instructions in *Legal-Wise* should help consumers produce completed documents that are accepted by court clerks.

Disclaimer
"This book is designed to provide accurate and authoritative information with respect to the subject matter covered. It is sold with the understanding that the publisher is not engaged in rendering legal or other professional services. If legal advice or other expert assistance is required, the services of a competent attorney

or other professional person should be sought. While
every attempt was made to provide accurate information,
the author or publisher cannot be held accountable for
errors or omissions."

Overall   **Grade: B⁺**

For the do-it-yourself consumer who wants a brief, accurate and inexpensive guide to legal issues and basic legal
forms, at $18.95 ***Legal-Wise: Self-Help Legal Guide for
Everyone*** is an exceptional value. It is also a good starting point for consumers who will want to buy more
detailed products as the need arises.

Recommended.

LEGAL LetterWorks

by Charles B. Chernofsky & Griffith G. deNoyelles, Jr.
Round Lake Publishing, Ridgefield, Connecticut, 1998
558 pages, PC or Mac Disk, $79.95
(203) 438-5255

Recommended

LEGAL LetterWorks is designed to help consumers deal with the many legal situations they encounter in their personal and business life. The book contains ten sections, each on a different legal need: Wills, Living Wills and Prenuptial Agreements; Buying, Selling and Leasing Real Estate; Buying and Selling Goods; Borrowing and Lending Money; Starting a Business; Operating a Corporation; Buying and Selling a Business; Contract Clauses and Notices; Employees and Representatives; Releases, Powers of Attorney and Notary Statements. This publication is not for use in Louisiana.

The forms and letters provided with *LetterWorks* will help you to write a will, rent a house or apartment, sell your car, prepare an employee contract, write a consulting agreement and many other legal tasks. Each section of the book features an introduction that describes the forms in it and each form or letter describes the appropriate situation for its use. A warning section for each form or letter discusses possible differences between states and other areas to be careful with. A floppy disk accompanies the book (available in both PC and Mac versions) that contain all of the forms and letters in ASCII files that can be used with any word processor.

Accuracy   **Grade: B⁻**

Although *LetterWorks* provides accurate and detailed legal forms and letters for a variety of situations, it does not discuss the law that applies to these forms.

Comprehensiveness   **Grade: A⁻**
It would be impossible to provide every form or letter
required for every legal situation. Even so, **LetterWorks**
provides the necessary forms and letters that most people
and new businesses will need in the most common situations.

Plain Language and Glossary   **Grade: B⁺**
LetterWorks avoids almost all legalese in the instructions,
but uses a great deal of legal terminology in its forms.
All legal terms are, however, clearly explained in the text
that accompanies each form or letter, and **LetterWorks**
contains a good glossary of definitions of the legal terms
it uses.

Easy to Use   **Grade: B**
LetterWorks is well-organized and takes you through the
process of using its forms and letters in a step-by-step fashion. Each form has an introduction that explains the form,
helps you determine if it is the correct form, and provides instructions for every blank on the form. This
ensures that you understand each and every part of the
form and avoid confusion. In each section, the book provides special information for troublesome areas, such as
retirement plans and married couples, and cautions the
reader in areas that might pose potential problems in filing. The included computer disk allows you to edit forms
on your word processor. This allows you to edit, cut,
paste and make any other changes to the form for your
situation. This is especially helpful when adding clauses
(also included in this product) to a document such as a
will. Otherwise you must re-type the document.

Red Flags   **Grade: B⁺**
LetterWorks contains a warning section before each form
or letter which informs on the possibility of state differences or other possible troublesome areas on the forms

and recommends you have your work reviewed by a local attorney when necessary.

Quality of Legal Forms **Grade: B⁺**

LetterWorks provides 215 forms and letters on numerous topics. The forms in the book are not for actual use because they are not of legal size and contain the detailed step-by-step instructions for filling them out. Instead you must use the included form disk (which has all of the forms and letters in a universal ASCII format) on your computer's word processor.

Disclaimer

"While no book can be a substitute for an attorney, many of the forms in this book cover basic situations and may not necessarily require an attorney's involvement. Others, of a more complex nature, can be completed by you but should be reviewed by an attorney. Still others cover technical areas and are included primarily for informational purposes. In these cases, an attorney should prepare the forms, but you will have the advantage of knowing what should be included."

Overall **Grade: B⁺**

For the person with a computer who would like a collection of legal forms and letters for most common situations they will come across, *LEGAL LetterWorks* is an excellent source with easy-to-follow instructions. Even with its hefty $79.95 price tag, *LEGAL LetterWorks* is a good value for the do-it-yourselfer with a home computer who wants a comprehensive collection of form letters and legal documents covering a wide, wide range of possible legal problems.

Recommended.

The Complete Book of Personal Legal Forms
2nd Edition
by Daniel Sitarz
Nova Publishing, Carbondale, Illinois, 1997
253 pages, PC or Mac Disk, $29.95
(800) 748-1175   **Good Value**

The Complete Book of Personal Legal Forms includes over 100 forms covering contracts, powers of attorney, notarial transactions, wills, living wills, living trusts, pre-marital agreements, marital settlement agreements, releases, receipts, rental agreements for real and personal property, personal loan documents, promissory notes and collection documents. In its selection, *Personal Legal Forms* also provides 13 miscellaneous business documents, including a request for credit information and a request to stop payment on a check. A PC form disk also comes with the publication.

Accuracy   **Grade: B⁻**

   Personal Legal Forms provides an accurate, but very brief overview of the general legal areas it covers. Individual legal forms are introduced in slightly more detail. While technically accurate, the forms are very basic and filled with legalese.

Comprehensiveness   **Grade: B**

   Personal Legal Forms does a good job of targeting the areas that are most important to most consumers: estate planning, real estate, family law and selling personal property. In some chapters a variety of forms are given (for example, four different kinds of powers of attorney), in other chapters, one key form (such as a general contract) is grouped with forms that extend, amend or revoke it.

Information about how to complete the forms varies greatly depending on which chapter you're reading. For the simple, fill-in-the-blank "boilerplate" forms (contract, releases and powers of attorney) little, if any, instruction is given. For example, in the book's general contract form between two parties, consumers are expected to fill in the details of the agreement without any instruction or descriptive examples. The disk provides forms in ASCII that are retrievable on both PCs and Macs. Worksheets, questionnaires and checklists are included in some of the chapters.

Plain Language and Glossary   **Grade: C**

Personal Legal Forms uses plain language in the text, but its forms are filled with legalese. Although a glossary of legal terms is included, it does not define many of the legal terms used in the book, such as vacate, lien, and release.

Easy to Use   **Grade: C**

Personal Legal Forms does not include step-by-step instructions for most of its forms. This may be because many of the forms are brief (only a page long) and fairly self-explanatory. Even so, there are times when consumers are expected to describe people, places, property or events–important contract language–without guidance or sample language. The addition of a form disk to this publication makes it much easier to generate forms. People without computers are urged to retype the entire form on 8.5 x 11 white paper.

Red Flags   **Grade: B**

Personal Legal Forms includes warnings about when legal help should be sought or when state law may vary, but the warnings are not presented in any obvious way such as boldface, capital lettering, special icons or other markings to help ensure that they are found be readers.

Quality of Legal Forms   **Grade: A**
   Personal Legal Forms includes forms that can easily
   be photocopied, retyped or computer-generated by
   do-it-yourselfers.

Disclaimer
   "Because of possible unanticipated changes in governing
   statutes and case law relating to the application of any information contained in this book, the author, publisher,
   and any and all persons or entities involved in any way in
   the preparation, publication, sale or distribution of this
   book disclaim all responsibility for the legal effects or consequences of any document prepared or action taken in
   reliance upon information contained in this book. No
   representations, either express or implied, are made or
   given regarding the legal consequences of the use of any
   information contained in this book. Purchasers and persons intending to use this book for the preparation of any
   legal documents are advised to check specifically on the
   current applicable laws in any jurisdiction in which they
   intend the documents to be effective."

Overall   **Grade: B**
   The Complete Book of Personal Legal Forms provides
   basic forms that could be made more useful with just a
   bit more instruction. For those new to the do-it-yourself
   movement, we recommend publications with more step-
   by-step instructions. At $29.95, **Personal Legal Forms**
   is for experienced and sophisticated consumers.

                              Good Value.

Not Recommended

Do-It-Yourself Assorted Legal Forms
SJT Enterprises, Inc., Cleveland, Ohio, 1997
Form Kit, $9.95
(800) 326-7419

Do-It-Yourself Assorted Legal Forms claims that it provides
"the most commonly requested legal forms written in easy to
understand language...." This means 16 forms that you can copy
out of the book and use, and over 250 forms on a floppy disk.
Less than minimal guidance is provided in the six sentences of
instruction on how to fill out the forms. The forms on the
floppy disk are in ASCII text format which is readable by any
word processor on any computer.

Accuracy   **Grade: C**
   Assorted Legal Forms provides legal forms for a variety
   of situations. The forms are generic, but accurate for the
   most basic situations they cover. No information is provided on the laws which the forms address.

Comprehensiveness   **Grade: C**
   Assorted Legal Forms provides the basic forms that most
   people and businesses will need for many common situations. The kit tends to concentrates on business forms,
   however, with only a limited selection of personal forms.

Plain Language and Glossary   **Grade: C**
   Assorted Legal Forms generally avoids the use of legalese
   and provides the forms in easy-to-understand language.
   Legal terminology is used, however, in many of the forms.
   The book does not contain a glossary, nor does it explain
   the terms in text.

Easy to Use   **Grade: F**
   Assorted Legal Forms will be difficult to use for those
without any experience in filling out legal forms. Only
six sentences of instructions are included which boil down
to "fill in the blanks and sign." No specific instructions
are provided for each form, nor is any other assistance
presented in this publication.

Red Flags   **Grade: F**
   Assorted Legal Forms does not address the possibility
of variations of the law in different states or provide any
warnings for areas that may cause problems.

Quality of Legal Forms   **Grade: B**
   Assorted Legal Forms provides 16 forms that are clearly
printed and suitable for copying, and a computer disk with
250 forms that may be used with any word processor to
make a nicely-printed document.

Disclaimer
   "It should be your understanding that this kit is not a substitute for legal advice. If you need legal advice, the
services of an attorney should be obtained."

Overall   **Grade: D**
   Do-It-Yourself Assorted Legal Forms should not be used
by consumers who do not already have experience in filling out legal forms, nor should it be used without
consulting other references that explain the law that applies to the forms it generates. Even at its modest $9.95
price tag, it is not a reasonable value for most do-it-
yourselfers.

Not Recommended.

The Legal Forms Kit
by Vijay Fadia
Homestead Publishing Company, Inc., Torrance, California,
1995
394 pages, $39.95
(213) 214-3559

Not Recommended

The Legal Forms Kit provides a large selection of legal forms
for the do-it-yourselfer. Over 180 forms are included with the
kit covering the following topics: real estate, leases and tenancies, loans and debts, credit and collections, sale of personal
property, partnership, employment, sale of goods, powers of
attorney, and personal (such as wills and prenuptial agreements). Minimal instructions are provided.

Accuracy   **Grade: C**
> *Legal Forms Kit* provides accurate and detailed legal
> forms and letters for a variety of situations. It provides
> minimal explanation of the law that applies to these forms.

Comprehensiveness   **Grade: B**
> It would be impossible to provide every form or letter
> required for every legal situation, but *Legal Forms Kit*
> provides the necessary forms and letters that most people
> and businesses will need in many common situations.

Plain Language and Glossary   **Grade: D**
> *Legal Forms Kit* uses legalese in many forms. Sometimes
> the language is explained, but often it is not. Generally
> the forms are clearly written and easy to understand, but
> the use of arcane wording makes them inaccessible to
> many consumers. The lack of a glossary leaves you on
> your own.

Easy to Use   **Grade: D**
Legal Forms Kit will be difficult to use for those without any experience in completing legal forms. Every
section begins with a brief introduction to the basic
legal concepts of the subject matter, but no instructions are given to assist in actually filling out the forms.
The lack of a forms disk will bother those who would
rather generate forms by computer.

Red Flags   **Grade: F**
Legal Forms Kit does not address variations of the law
in different states, nor does it provide any warnings for
areas that may cause problems.

Quality of Legal Forms   **Grade: B**
Legal Forms Kit provides over 180 forms that are clearly
printed and suitable for copying. The forms are perforated for easy removal.

Disclaimer
"Although care has been taken to ensure the accuracy and
utility of the information and forms contained in this
book, neither the publisher nor the author can in any way
guarantee that the forms are being used for the purposes
intended and therefore, assume no responsibility for their
proper and correct use. You must ascertain applicability
of various forms to the laws and customs of your local
jurisdiction. This publication is sold with the understanding that the publisher is not engaged in rendering legal,
accounting, or other professional service. Consult a
competent professional for answers to your specific
questions."

Overall   **Grade: D-**
The Legal Forms Kit should not be used by the consumer
who does not already have experience in completing legal forms, nor should it be used without consulting other

references that explain the law that applies to the forms it generates. At $39.95, it is not a reasonable value for most do-it-yourselfers.

Not Recommended.

301 Legal Forms and Agreements
E-Z Legal Forms, Inc., Deerfield Beach, Florida, 1993
282 pages, $24.95
(954) 480-8933

Not Recommended

A hard copy (no computer disks) collection, E-Z Legal's *301 Legal Forms and Agreements* covers basic agreements, loans and borrowing, employment, credit and collection, buying and selling, leases and tenancies, transfers and assignments, personal and family, real estate, and business. In addition to boilerplate, tear-out, fill-in-the-blank forms, *301* provides an eleven-page glossary of legal terms.

Accuracy   **Grade: D⁻**

301 Legal Forms provides "bare-bones" legal forms, which are often little more than a title, a few clauses and a signature line, and provides no legal discussion about the forms. The lack of any guidance, as well as the lack of any discussion of differences in individual states, are major gaps in *301*, which make it difficult for consumers to produce documents that are accurate and complete.

Comprehensiveness   **Grade: D**

Although *301 Legal Forms* contains many forms, it uses a "one-size-fits-all" approach that relies upon consumers to do substantial amounts of drafting on their own. While this approach works well for forms in areas such as consumer credit disputes and simple business documents, it does not work well for more complex areas such as wills and trusts, or real estate transactions. For individuals who are experienced in preparing forms, *301*'s "one-size-fits-all" approach may not be a problem, but for most consumers a better approach is to provide alternative language that covers different situations.

Plain Language and Glossary **Grade: F**

Many of the boilerplate forms included in *301 Legal Forms* include unnecessary legal terms and jargon. While legalese may make forms look more formal and official, it does not make them any more effective. Legalese is especially confusing and distracting in *301*, because it is not explained. The eleven-page glossary included in *301* often restates the titles of documents in slightly different language and provides little help to consumers trying to understand legal concepts.

Easy to Use **Grade: D‑**

301 Legal Forms includes both a topical table of contents and an alphabetical listing of all materials, which makes it easier to find a needed form. The lack of step-by-step instructions and absence of any explanations of the forms leaves consumers largely "on their own."

Red Flags **Grade: D‑**

Solely a form book, *301 Legal Forms* provides no explanations of the forms it includes or any discussion of possible hazards consumers should avoid. The few warnings we found in *301 Legal Forms* were like those in the text of the two-page Last Will and Testament: "Note: If your gross estate exceeds $600,000 ($1,200,000 for a married couple), consult an attorney. Caution: Louisiana residents should consult an attorney before preparing a will."

Quality of Legal Forms **Grade: D**

301 Legal Forms provides clearly-printed forms in a large typeface for fill-in-the-blank users. Since consumers will be drafting large amounts of text on their own, the one-page forms may not be adequate for many of the final documents consumers try to produce.

Disclaimer

"...As with any legal matter, common sense should determine whether you need the assistance of an attorney. We urge you to consult an attorney, qualified estate planner, or tax professional, or to seek other relevant expert advice whenever substantial sums of money are involved, you doubt the suitability of the product you have purchased, or if there is anything about the product you do not understand, including its adequacy to protect you. Even if you are completely satisfied with this product, we encourage you to have your attorney review it..."

Overall   **Grade: D**

E-Z Legal's ***301 Legal Forms and Agreements*** is more like the boilerplate form books found in many law libraries than a self-help publication. For experienced forms preparers, ***301*** may be a useful source for standard documents, but at $24.95, it is not a good value for either do-it-yourself consumers or those who are working with lawyers, independent paralegals or other professionals.

Not Recommended.

2

FAMILY LAW

Most people who hear the words "family law" automatically think "divorce law." And in truth, divorce and related issues (child custody, support and visitation rights) do make up most family law practice.

We have reviewed self-help products designed for a national audience that cover do-it-yourself divorce, child custody and support agreements, and premarital agreements. At the end of the chapter we also briefly look at products designed for gay and lesbian couples, and for non-married couples living together.

For help with other family law related issues, such as adoption, guardianships and name changes, please check the legal encyclopedias reviewed in Chapter 1.

All of the products we reviewed that cover family law issues are paper form books, so do-it-yourselfers have to depend on pre-computer technology—photocopies, typewriters and tear-out forms. But the important information is there and readily accessible.

DO-IT-YOURSELF DIVORCE

Recent statistics show that about 1.2 million divorces occur each year. Whether or not legal assistance is needed to get a divorce depends on the complexity of the issues involved and, of course, the divorcing couple.

If spouses approach divorce with the attitude that they will do what's right for *both* parties and any children, many divorces can be handled without a lawyer.

Even if one or two issues start out being contested, couples who successfully reach a settlement agreement on all issues (property division, child custody and support and visitation rights)—either on their own or with the help of a mediator—can proceed with a do-it-yourself divorce. Nova Publishing's *Divorce Yourself* stands out as the best resource for most do-it-yourself consumers who want to deal with divorce and avoid hiring a lawyer, and is a HALT Do-it-Yourself Best Buy.

CHILD CUSTODY AND SUPPORT AGREEMENTS

Divorcing couples who cannot voluntarily reach fair decisions about child custody, support and visitation will have a court make these decisions for them. This takes time and money, and in the long run, may not be satisfactory to either spouse or the children. It is much better for most couples to develop custody and parenting agreements—without court interference—that are comprehensive, long-lasting and in the best interest of the child. Again, Nova Publishing's *Divorce Yourself* stands out along with *Child Custody: Building Parenting Agreements That Work* from Nolo Press as the best comprehensive resources for do-it-yourselfers, and are HALT Do-it-Yourself Best Buys.

PREMARITAL AGREEMENTS

A couple can agree to change the usual rules about property ownership, and create their own in a contract they sign before the wedding that lays out the way matters will be handled at the end of the marriage whether through divorce or death.

Such an agreement is called a premarital or prenuptial

agreement. It's a contract between two people planning to marry that establishes the property rights each will have in the marriage, and what will happen should one die or the marriage end in divorce.

We recommend Sourcebooks Publishing's *How to Write Your Own Premarital Agreement* for do-it-yourselfers who want such a planning device.

Divorce Yourself:
The National No-Fault Divorce Kit
4th Edition
by Daniel Sitarz
Nova Publishing Co., Carbondale, Illinois, 1998
334 pages, $24.95
(800) 748-1175

Do-it-Yourself
Best Buy

Divorce Yourself: The National No-Fault Divorce Kit is
designed to allow you to prepare a no-fault divorce agreement
anywhere in the United States without hiring a lawyer. It
contains everything you need to know to handle your own
uncontested divorce, including division of property, alimony
and maintenance, income tax consequences, child custody and
visitation, child support, how to restore your former name, how
to prepare and file your own papers, and how to appear in court.
The book also contains easy-to-use legal forms with complete
instructions, detailed questionnaires, worksheets and checklists, courtroom guidelines, and a thorough guide to the divorce
laws in every state and the District of Columbia.

Accuracy   **Grade: A**
  Divorce Yourself contains thorough, accurate and detailed information on the process of divorce and the legal
  proceedings you will have to go through. The book provides an extensive discussion of divorce and tells you when
  you need to check the state law appendix for variations in
  your state's law.

Comprehensiveness   **Grade: A**
  Divorce Yourself provides all of the information you
  will need to file your own "no-fault" divorce, and will give
  you an excellent understanding of the process of divorce
  and the legal issues involved.

Plain Language and Glossary   **Grade: A⁺**

Divorce Yourself does an excellent job of avoiding the use of legalese and clearly explains any divorce terminology that must be used. It also contains an extensive glossary of legal definitions for easy reference.

Easy to Use   **Grade: B⁺**

Divorce Yourself is designed to be used in a step-by-step fashion. First, you and your spouse should read the entire book, so that you both fully understand the process. Each main section includes a questionnaire or worksheet, followed by a discussion of the law and general guidelines to assist the two of you in making decisions. ***Divorce Yourself*** also includes alternative language you can use in your divorce agreement, so you and your spouse can easily implement your decisions. ***Divorce Yourself*** then guides you through the process of assembling the individual clauses into a final divorce agreement. Instructions for signing, notarizing, and filing your agreement to get a no-fault divorce in your state are also included, as are examples of completed forms and a bibliography of divorce-related reference books.

Red Flags   **Grade: A**

Divorce Yourself includes prominent warnings about when you should check the detailed appendix of state divorce laws, check with the court clerk, or consult a law library for additional information not contained in the text. It also clearly tells you when you may need professional assistance to complete your divorce.

Quality of Legal Forms   **Grade: A⁻**

Divorce Yourself contains virtually every basic divorce form you may need, and identifies state-specific information in its state-by-state appendix. The forms are extremely clear and legible and are easily modified to include your state's information from the appendix. The lack of a computer disk is this product's biggest drawback.

Disclaimer

"Because of possible unanticipated changes in governing statutes and case law relating to the application of any information contained in this book, the author, publisher, and any and all persons or entities involved in any way in the preparation, publication, sale, or distribution of this book disclaim all responsibility for the legal effects or consequences of any document prepared or action taken in reliance upon information contained in this book. No representations, either express or implied, are made or given regarding the legal consequences of the use of any information contained in this book. Purchasers and persons intending to use this book for the preparation of any legal documents are advised to check specifically on the current applicable laws in any jurisdiction in which they intend the documents to be effective. This book is not printed, published, sold, circulated, or distributed with the intention that it be used to procure or aid in the procurement of any legal effect or ruling in any jurisdiction in which such procurement or aid may be restricted by statute."

Overall   **Grade: A**

At \$24.95, ***Divorce Yourself*** is an exceptional value that provides a very thorough resource for do-it-yourself consumers who need an uncontested no-fault divorce.

HALT
Do-it-Yourself
Best Buy

Child Custody:
Building Parenting Agreements That Work
2nd Edition
by Mimi E. Lyster
Nolo Press, Berkeley, California, 1996
208 pages, $24.95
(800) 992-6656

HALT
Do-it-Yourself
Best Buy

Child Custody: Building Parenting Agreements That Work, assists parents in creating fair child custody and visitation agreements that are comprehensive, long-lasting, and in the best interests of the children. It includes a thorough explanation of legal and practical information you should know to negotiate and create a child custody agreement, even in high conflict situations. *Child Custody* also includes a series of worksheets, with step-by-step instructions that provide all the information you need to complete the included child custody agreement, as well as numerous charts that show how your state's laws affect your situation.

Accuracy   **Grade: A**
 Child Custody contains a thorough and accurate discussion of legal principles and practical considerations that affect your child custody and visitation decisions. The book provides very detailed information and clearly warns you when you need to check state laws or to consult an attorney.

Comprehensiveness   **Grade: A**
 Child Custody contains all the information you need to create a thorough agreement. It covers health care, education, religion, living arrangements, holidays, moving away, decision-making, dispute resolution, and different parenting styles. *Child Custody* also guides you through

the negotiation process, helping you identify your
needs and concerns, minimizing conflicts, and negotiating money issues. Other topics covered include
multicultural, step and adoptive families, using mediation or arbitration, and other adult relationship
issues such as dating and remarriage. Charts containing information on different state rules appear
throughout the book, so you can see how your state's
laws affect your situation.

Plain Language and Glossary   **Grade: A⁻**
  Child Custody does an excellent job of avoiding the use
of legalese, and clearly explains in the text any legal terminology that must be used. The one shortcoming of
Child Custody is the lack of a glossary that defines legal
terminology.

Easy to Use   **Grade: A**
  Child Custody is designed to be easy to use in a step-by-
step fashion. First, both parents should read the book, so
they are fully informed and understand the decisions they
make regarding their children. Second, the worksheets
should be completed. Finally, the information gathered
from the worksheets is used to fill in the blanks of the
parenting agreement. Step-by-step instructions are included to assist you in completing the forms. Your final
document should also be adjusted based on the laws of
your state, which are pointed out throughout the text in
the state law charts. If you would rather write your own
agreement, this is easily accomplished using the information you've collected from the worksheets and the
knowledge you've gained by reading the book.

Red Flags   **Grade: A**
  Child Custody includes prominent warnings that alert
the reader when state laws vary, and provides additional
detailed information in an accompanying chart. It also

clearly identifies complex situations when an attorney or other professional may be necessary.

Quality of Legal Forms **Grade: A⁻**

The forms are of excellent quality and make excellent copies. They are perforated for easy removal and use. The lack of a computer forms disk is, however, a drawback.

Disclaimer

"We've done our best to give you useful and accurate information in this book. But laws and procedures change frequently and are subject to differing interpretations. If you want legal advice backed by a guarantee, see a lawyer. If you use this book, it's your responsibility to make sure that the facts and general advice contained in it are applicable to your situation."

Overall **Grade: A**

At $24.95, *Child Custody: Building Parenting Agreements That Work* is an exceptional value that provides consumers with a very thorough resource for creating their own child custody and visitation agreements.

HALT
Do-it-Yourself
Best Buy

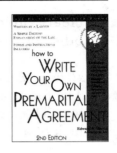

How to Write Your Own Premarital Agreement

2nd Edition
by Edward A. Haman
Sourcebooks, Inc., Naperville, Illinois, 1998
175 pages, $19.95
(800) 226-5291

Recommended

How to Write Your Own Premarital Agreement provides thorough information, step-by-step instructions, and fill-in-the-blank forms for preparing a premarital agreement. The book also includes state laws that govern premarital agreements, a glossary of terms and a copy of the Uniform Premarital Agreement Act. Chapter 4, The Law of Premarital Agreements, explains the legal principles courts use to make decisions about property distribution, child custody and support issues. Real-life examples help to drive home the author's points. A short chapter entitled Talking to Your Partner deals with the sometimes sticky subject of getting your betrothed to agree to a prenuptial agreement. The final chapter tells you how to select and work with a lawyer if you need professional assistance.

Premarital Agreement includes two basic forms—one for couples who have roughly equal assets and another, which can be customized through the selection of alternative clauses, for those with more complex finances. Easy to understand step-by-step instructions for completing the premarital agreement and related forms (for example, financial statements, schedules of joint and separate property) are also included.

Accuracy   **Grade: A**
  Premarital Agreement provides thorough, accurate and up-to-date information about creating a legally-valid document. It also includes divorce and probate laws for each state, and a guide to states that have adopted the Uniform Premarital Agreement Act.

Comprehensiveness   **Grade: B⁺**

Premarital Agreement provides a thorough discussion
of premarital agreements and when they are most often
used. Missing is a balanced discussion of whether a premarital agreement is really needed. Although a chapter is
devoted to that question, the author argues that even young
people with minimal assets who are marrying for the first
time should consider an agreement, because "there is some
evidence to indicate that premarital agreements actually
promote stability in a marriage."

Plain Language and Glossary   **Grade: B**

The text is generally written in plain language, but the
forms include quite a bit of legal jargon and terminology.
Premarital Agreements includes a glossary of legal
terms that defines most, but not all, legal terms used in
the book.

Easy to Use   **Grade: B⁺**

This book is easy to understand and use. Explicit and
easy to follow step-by-step directions are included for completing, signing, witnessing and notarizing the forms.

Red Flags   **Grade: B⁻**

State laws are included, as well as information on how to
do your own legal research and how to find a lawyer.
There are no warnings, however, about potential pitfalls
in drafting or specific situations that might require expert
help.

Quality of Legal Forms   **Grade: B**

The agreements are easy to execute and can be customized to fit individual circumstances. The finished product
is a completed preprinted form, which should be fully adequate for most consumers.

Disclaimer
    "This publication is designed to provide accurate and authoritative information in regard to the subject matter covered. It is sold with the understanding that the publisher is not engaged in rendering legal, accounting, or other professional services. If legal advice or other expert assistance is required, the services of a competent professional person should be sought."

Overall   **Grade: B⁺**

    *At $19.95, **Premarital Agreement** is* an excellent value for couples who agree that they need a premarital agreement and who have done their homework to ensure that their interests are protected.

                                           Recommended.

How to File Your Own Divorce

3rd Edition
by Edward A. Haman
Sourcebooks, Inc., Naperville, Illinois, 1998
238 pages, $19.95
(800) 226-5291

Recommended

How to File Your Own Divorce will allow do-it-yourself consumers to obtain a divorce without hiring a lawyer, or work more effectively with a lawyer if they do choose to hire one. This product thoroughly explains the process of divorce and how you can handle it yourself, including the following topics: how to file for divorce, separation and annulment, uncontested and contested divorce, simplified procedures for some states, when you need a lawyer, how to find and work with one, grounds for divorce, property division, alimony, child support, child custody, visitation, protecting your assets, and court procedures.

How to File also includes a sample case with completed forms, as well as a detailed state-by-state summary of divorce laws with citations, so you can find them easily in your state's statute books when you do your own research.

Accuracy   **Grade: B**

How to File contains an accurate, but somewhat general, explanation of divorce and the legal process you have to go through. The book clearly indicates when state specific rules deviate from the general information it discusses, and provides a summary of state rules.

Comprehensiveness   **Grade: B**

How to File provides an excellent summary and explanation of almost every topic that may come to mind when you're involved in a divorce. The book helps you understand and navigate the divorce process, and provides insights about how judges tend to view divorce cases. Completing the forms correctly for your state, however, may require some additional research.

Plain Language and Glossary   Grade: B⁻

How to File avoids almost all legalese, and provides some general explanations of divorce terminology in the text. It does not contain a glossary that defines divorce terminology.

Easy to Use   Grade: B

How to File is well-designed and straightforward to use. First, you read the text to understand the process, then you follow the chapters in a sequential fashion. Each chapter also includes detailed instructions on how to complete forms and worksheets. The 15 forms included in this product are general, however, and require you to consult the detailed information contained in the summary of your state's laws to make any necessary changes.

Red Flags   Grade: A

How to File contains special caution boxes and other warnings when information should be double-checked against the laws of your jurisdiction (in the appendix or with research in a law library), and alerts you when the services of a professional might be necessary.

Quality of Legal Forms   Grade: B⁺

The 15 forms included in *How to File* cover the information required in most jurisdictions, are clear, and will produce excellent photocopies, but are not perforated for easy removal.

Disclaimer

"This publication is designed to provide accurate and authoritative information in regard to the subject matter covered. It is sold with the understanding that the publisher is not engaged in rendering legal, accounting, or other professional service. If legal advice or other expert assistance is required, the services of a competent professional person should be sought."

Overall **Grade: B**

At $19.95, *How to File Your Own Divorce* is a good resource for consumers who wish to handle their own divorce, work better with an attorney, or simply want a good summary of the divorce process.

Recommended.

Do-It-Yourself No-fault Divorce Kit
SJT Enterprises, Inc., Cleveland, Ohio, 1998
Form Kit, $24.95
(800) 326-7419

Not Recommended

Do-It-Yourself No-fault Divorce Kit comes with three
separate booklets: a Step-by-Step Instructional Guide; Law and
Requirements in all 50 states and Washington, DC; and Practice
Worksheets. The kit also provides separate preprinted forms
for filing an uncontested divorce in court, a form disk and a
"money-back guarantee." It provides a general discussion about
how to complete various sections of the kit's marital settlement
agreement. State-by-state information is also included, which
cites the law concerning divorce and specific language requirements for each state.

Accuracy   **Grade: D**
   No-fault Divorce Kit provides accurate, but less than
   bare-bones information on no-fault divorce. The lack of
   detail can be dangerous for those who would rely solely
   on this kit.

Comprehensiveness   **Grade: D⁻**
   No-fault Divorce Kit barely skims the surface of every
   topic it addresses. Most shocking is its advice on property distribution, "Generally, all items should be divided
   equally." The ***Kit*** fails to mention, let alone explain, what
   laws govern property division or discuss the differences
   between "community property" states like California and
   others which require "equitable distribution." Nor does
   the ***Kit*** provide any assistance, in the way of questionnaires

or worksheets, that helps you figure out exactly what is owned, how it's owned, and in whose name(s).

Plain Language and Glossary **Grade: C**

The text and fill-in-the blank documents are written primarily in plain language, but are so limited that there is no call for using legal terminology. *No-fault Divorce Kit* does not include a glossary of legal terms.

Easy to Use **Grade: D**

Instead of providing step-by-step instructions, this kit provides a completed sample marital settlement agreement, and tells you to select the correct circled letters to insert clauses that correspond to information in the state-by-state appendix. This extremely awkward approach is no substitute for step-by-step guidance.

Red Flags **Grade: D**

The book does not alert you to possible problems in any obvious way. For example, one important caution is buried in the *No-fault Divorce Kit's* opening money-back guarantee letter, which tells you that some jurisdictions require local forms in addition to the forms it provides.

Quality of Legal Forms **Grade: D**

One set of pre-printed, easy to read and fill-in forms is included as worksheets, and another as the original to file with the courthouse. The reader can type the original forms after practicing on the worksheets, and produce forms that are suitable for filing. A form disk was apparently added after the kit was published, but is not discussed in any of the printed materials.

The publisher offers a money-back guarantee and half the court costs if the court refuses to accept their forms. However, to get your money back you have to meet five requirements, some fairly arduous, including getting a letter from the judge "explaining why your case was not accepted."

Disclaimer

"This material is sold with the understanding that neither the author or the publisher is engaged in rendering legal advice. If legal advice is needed, the services of an attorney should be obtained. BY FILLING OUT THE FORMS IN THIS BOOK, YOU ARE ACTING AS YOUR OWN ATTORNEY. The author and/or publisher of this book and forms are not liable for material in this publication."

Overall   **Grade: D**

At $24.95, ***Do-it-Yourself No-fault Divorce Kit*** is an overly-simplified product that can be dangerous for do-it-yourself legal consumers.

Not Recommended.

Recommended Reading

The Living Together Kit: A Legal Guide for Unmarried Couples
by Toni Ihara & Ralph Warner, Nolo Press, 8th Edition, 1997, 240 pages.
$24.95

A reference and do-it-yourself legal guide for unmarried couples who live together, *The Living Together Kit* provides the latest information on how rules and regulations affect the rights of unmarried co-habitants in property ownership, parenthood, insurance coverage, social security eligibility, separation and death. A variety of "living together" fill-in-the-blank contracts are provided at the end of the book for unmarried couples who want to protect their legal rights. This kit provides the same in-depth coverage you find in other Nolo Press products, and includes sample contracts, helpful charts and an extensive index.

A Legal Guide for Lesbian and Gay Couples
by Hayden Curry, Denis Clifford and Robin Leonard, Nolo Press, 9th Edition,
1996, 344 pages. $24.95

The recently-updated edition of *A Legal Guide for Lesbian and Gay Couples* reflects numerous changes in the laws regarding gay men and lesbians. Complete with real-life examples of how individual gays have fared when challenging various laws, the guide includes up-to-date information, step-by-step instructions and fill-in-the-blank legal forms for living together agreements, durable powers of attorney, wills, parenting agreements, and property ownership agreements—all tailored to meet the special legal needs of gay men and lesbians.

3

PROPERTY RIGHTS

We call the places we live many things, a roof over my head, house, condo, townhouse, apartment, flat, crib. These places are all "real property" that you either own or rent. We all need one and have to go through the hoops of becoming an owner or tenant. And some of us eventually become sellers or landlords. In all of these dealings ask yourself, "Do I really need a lawyer for this, or can I do it myself?"

This chapter reviews products that cover renting or leasing an apartment or a single family home. This is an area that does not often require the use of a lawyer. After all, when was the last time you hired a lawyer to look over a lease before you signed it?

But did you carefully read what you were signing? Probably not, and you might not have understood all the legal "mumbo-jumbo" anyway. After reading a good self-help book that explains what goes into a rental agreement or lease, you will understand what you're being asked to sign, and will know whether you want to make any changes.

Although a lawyer is not usually necessary in most dealings between a landlord and tenant, both sides should know what they're getting into by having basic knowledge of the legal aspects of renting and leasing property. That's where these do-it-yourself books come into play. By knowing and understanding the legal rights and responsibilities of both a landlord and a tenant, both parties can protect themselves.

When it comes to buying or selling a house or condo, although you can often do it all yourself, many states require you to hire a lawyer or other real estate professional to complete the sale. The good news is that you do not need a lawyer for the entire process, but only at the closing.

The self-help books reviewed in this chapter also cover buying and selling a home. These helpful books provide thorough background on the buying and selling process, and after reading one of them you'll know if you need a lawyer or other real estate professional and to what extent.

Every Tenant's Legal Guide, Every Landlord's Legal Guide, and *Quick and Legal Leases & Rental Agreements,* all from Nolo Press are HALT Do-it-Yourself Best Buys. To purchase a home, we recommend Sourcebook's *How to Buy a Condominium or Townhouse.*

Every Tenant's Legal Guide
2nd Edition
by Janet Portman and Marcia Stewart
Nolo Press, Berkeley, California, 1997
350 pages, $24.95
(800) 992-6656

HALT
Do-it-Yourself
Best Buy

Every Tenant's Legal Guide covers virtually everything you need to know when it comes to the tenant's side of renting or leasing an apartment or house. It contains all of the legal and practical information you need to deal with your landlord and to protect your rights if things go wrong. Starting with how to find the right apartment, *Every Tenant's Legal Guide* thoroughly covers getting your security deposit back, eviction and everything in between.

Accuracy   **Grade: A**
   Every Tenant's Legal Guide presents thorough, accurate, and detailed information about renting or leasing an apartment or house.

Comprehensiveness   **Grade: A**
   Every Tenant's Legal Guide is extremely detailed and thoroughly covers renting or leasing your home. Every question you may have appears to be addressed, including how to find and inspect an apartment, fair and legal lease agreements, roommates, rent increases, late rent, security deposits, rent control, repairs, privacy rights, discrimination, environmental hazards (such as lead and asbestos), ending or breaking a lease, eviction, security, safety, landlord responsibilities, and small claims court actions. If your landlord provides forms, they should be compared with the ones in this guide to identify areas where the landlord may be trying to take advantage of you.

Every Tenant's Legal Guide also includes appendices covering the laws that affect tenants and citations so you can do additional research yourself. It also lists state agencies that may be able to help you if you have a problem with your landlord or the premises, and includes information on how to use a lawyer and how to represent yourself in small claims court.

Plain Language and Glossary   Grade: A⁻

Written in plain language, *Every Tenant's Legal Guide* effectively avoids almost all legalese. Any remaining legal terminology is explained in the text. The one shortcoming of *Every Tenant's Legal Guide* is the lack of a glossary.

Easy to Use   Grade: A

Every Tenant's Legal Guide is straightforward and easy to use. It is laid out chronologically from shopping for an apartment to moving out (including any possible lawsuits). Simply read the sections on your situation and use the included forms.

Red Flags   Grade: A

Every Tenant's Legal Guide covers differences in state laws through thorough appendices, and warns you when you may wish to consult an attorney or do additional legal research yourself.

Quality of Legal Forms   Grade: A

The 10 forms and worksheets provided with *Every Tenant's Legal Guide* are clear, will produce excellent photocopies, and are perforated for easy removal from the book.

Disclaimer

"We've done our best to give you useful and accurate information in this book. But laws and procedures change frequently and are subject to differing interpretations. If you want legal advice backed by a guarantee, see a lawyer. If you use this book, it's your responsibility to make sure that the facts and general advice contained in it are applicable to your situation."

Overall **Grade: A**

Every Tenant's Legal Guide is an extraordinary product; you won't be able to find a better tenant's guide for renting or leasing an apartment or house at any price. At $24.95, *Every Tenant's Legal Guide* is an exceptional value for anyone who rents.

HALT
Do-it-Yourself
Best Buy

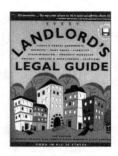

Every Landlord's Legal Guide
2nd Edition
by Marcia Stewart, Ralph Warner & Janet Portman
Nolo Press, Berkeley, California, 1997
496 pages, $34.95
(800) 992-6656

HALT
Do-it-Yourself
Best Buy

Every Landlord's Legal Guide is a reference book for landlords and property managers. It offers a detailed discussion of the laws governing the landlord/tenant relationship. Chapters include screening tenants, preparing leases and rental agreements, basic rent rules, security deposits, discrimination, property managers, getting the tenant moved in, co-tenants, sublets and assignments, landord's duty to repair and maintain the premises, landlord's liability for dangerous conditions, landlord's liability for environmental health hazards, landlord's liability for criminal acts and activities, landlord's right of entry and tenant's privacy, ending a tenancy, returning security deposits, problems with tenants, terminations and evictions, and lawyers and legal research. *Every Landlord's Legal Guide* also includes information and step-by-step instructions for preparing a lease or rental agreement, tear-out forms, a computer disk, state laws and agencies, and an index.

Accuracy   **Grade: A**

Every Landlord's Legal Guide offers comprehensive and accurate information on landlord/tenant law. Appendices provide landlord/tenant statutes for each state as well as state breakdowns on rent rules, security deposits, lead hazard reduction laws, termination for nonpayment, and termination for violation of lease. Information on how to do your own legal research is also included.

Comprehensiveness **Grade: A⁺**

Every Landlord's Legal Guide is a hefty book (496 pages long) with 18 chapters and 27 "fill-in-the-blank" forms, letters, agreements and checklists.

The amount of detail in this book—given that landlord/tenant laws vary from state to state—is truly amazing. In addition to a detailed discussion of the major issues that arise between landlords and tenants (such as executing leases and rental agreements, and the laws governing security deposits), ***Every Landlord's Legal Guide*** offers guidance on a whole host of issues that may come up during the relationship, such as what to do if a tenant makes improvements to an apartment without prior authorization. There is also a chapter on hiring and supervising property managers.

Throughout the book, you will find useful "real-life" examples that help illustrate various points. The use of charts, graphics, screened boxed information and white space on almost every page makes the book not only easy on the eyes but a pleasure to read.

The step-by-step instructions for filling out the leases and rental agreements are easy to follow, and the computer disk makes it easy to complete the forms in the book.

Plain Language and Glossary **Grade: A⁻**

The text and fill-in-the blank documents are written in plain language. Legalese is used only when necessary and is explained in the text. A glossary of legal terms is not included, however.

Easy to Use **Grade: A⁺**

Every Landlord's Legal Guide is extremely easy to read and follow. Each of the book's fill-in-the-blank forms is explained in detail, and leases and rental agreements are even explained clause by clause. A sample of each form is also completed to show you how to fill it out.

Red Flags   **Grade: A**
Areas that warrant special attention are flagged with special icons, and *Every Landlord's Legal Guide* clearly tells you when you may need to contact a lawyer, when other resources should be consulted, and when you can skip or skim a section.

Quality of Legal Forms   **Grade: B⁺**

Quality of Legal Forms   **Grade: B+**
The forms are easily photocopied and completed or computer generated. The form disk is formatted for the PC (MS-DOS), and can be used by any PC running Windows or DOS. If you use a Mac, you must have PC Exchange software (which is now built into the operating system). The formatting of the forms on disk has been simplified, so you may have to reformat them with your word processor to get the forms to look like the ones in the book.

Disclaimer
"We've done our best to give you useful and accurate information in this book. But laws and procedures change frequently and are subject to differing interpretations. If you want legal advice backed by a guarantee, see a lawyer. If you use this book, it's your responsibility to make sure that the facts and general advice contained in it are applicable to your situation."

Overall   **Grade: A**
Every Landlord's Legal Guide is a one-of-a-kind reference tool for landlords. Although landlords are advised to find a trustworthy lawyer to help them when problems arise, many will find that all they really need is this book. At $34.95, why would any landlord be without one?

HALT
Do-it-Yourself
Best Buy

Leases & Rental Agreements

1st Edition
by Marcia Stewart & Ralph Warner
Nolo Press, Berkeley, California, 1996
160 pages, $18.95
(800) 992-6656

HALT
Do-it-Yourself
Best Buy

Leases & Rental Agreements provides thorough background information, step-by-step instructions and fill-in-the-blank forms for creating a lease or rental agreement. Chapters include Choosing Tenants, Getting the Tenants Moved In, and Changing or Ending a Tenancy. Sample fill-in agreements, state-specific appendices and an index are also included.

Accuracy   Grade: **A**
   Leases & Rental Agreements provides a thorough, accurate and complete overview of the law governing leases and rental agreements to help landlords understand what they are and are not permitted to do. State statutes governing these agreements and the landlord/tenant relationship are included for each state.

Comprehensiveness   **Grade: A**
   Leases & Rental Agreements includes an excellent discussion of how to draft a legally valid lease or rental agreement. Easy to follow step-by-step instructions are provided as well as information on how documents can be modified to fit various circumstances. Important landlord/tenant relationship issues are covered to help landlords avoid legal troubles like a discrimination lawsuit. The book contains a number of different tables listing state statutes governing security deposits and notice requirements

for terminating a tenancy. It also includes other useful forms for landlords such as a rental application, consent to background and reference checks, tenant references, and a landlord/tenant checklist on the general condition of the rooms.

Plain Language and Glossary   **Grade: A⁻**

Plain language is used in the text and the forms. Legal terms are used only when necessary. A glossary of legal terms is not included, however.

Easy to Use   **Grade: B⁺**

Leases & Rental Agreements includes excellent step-by-step instructions for completing its forms along with details on what each clause means and how to use it. The reader can also consult sample documents, worksheets and letters in the text.

A computer disk (which is not included) would allow users to generate professional-looking forms more quickly. Landlords who want to make sure their agreements comply with state laws should visit a local law library and read their state statute (cited at the back of the book).

Red Flags   **Grade: A**

Areas that warrant special attention are flagged with special icons. Readers are told when they may need to contact a lawyer, when other resources should be consulted, whether they can skip or skim a section and more.

Quality of Legal Forms   **Grade: B⁺**

Leases & Rental Agreements contains a set of perforated fill-in-the-blank forms. The forms are easily photocopied and completed. In some, like the rental agreement and residential lease, you have a series of clause options to choose from, so your final form, if not completely retyped, will include filled-in blanks and check marks.

Disclaimer

"We've done our best to give you useful and accurate information in this book. But laws and procedures change frequently and are subject to differing interpretations. If you want legal advice backed by a guarantee, see a lawyer. If you use this book, it's your responsibility to make sure that the facts and general advice contained in it are applicable to your situation."

Overall **Grade: A**

This is an extremely easy to use do-it-yourself tool for residential landlords. The references to state law and forms that can be photocopied and used over and over again gives this book a long shelf life. At $18.95, ***Leases & Rental Agreements*** is an exceptional value.

HALT
Do-it-Yourself
Best Buy

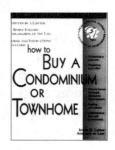

How to Buy a Condominium or Townhome

by Irwin E. Leiter
Sourcebooks, Inc., Naperville, Illinois, 1997
166 pages, $16.95
(800) 226-5291

Recommended

How to Buy a Condominium or Townhome is a step-by-step guide that provides the information you need to know to avoid problems in purchasing a home. The book covers almost every aspect of the purchase and explains types of real estate ownership, owners' associations, how to find the right property, determining what you can afford, maintenance fees and assessments, how to inspect property, using real estate brokers and agents, purchase documents, closing, privacy concerns, seller's disclosure requirements, and general information on condo or townhome living. ***How to Buy*** also contains sample forms and worksheets, and a state-by-state reference guide to laws for all 50 states and the District of Columbia.

Accuracy   **Grade: B**
   How to Buy provides accurate and thorough information about purchasing this type of real estate. The book will refer you to the state reference section whenever it is applicable or necessary.

Comprehensiveness   **Grade: B**
   How to Buy is a very informative reference guide that covers most topics you will need to know in purchasing a condo or townhome. The book will take you through the process step-by-step, and includes a state-by-state citation list of state laws that may affect your purchase. A summary of the most important state laws that may affect your purchase would have been a good addition, however.

Plain Language and Glossary   **Grade: A**

How to Buy avoids almost all legalese, and defines any remaining real estate terminology in a glossary of definitions that is included in a special section of the introduction.

Easy to Use   **Grade: A**

How to Buy is straightforward and easy to use. First, you should read the entire text so you understand the important background information. Then just go through the book section by section, filling out the worksheets and forms as needed. Excellent step-by-step instructions and explanations are provided to guide you through each form and worksheet.

Red Flags   **Grade: B**

How to Buy points out any area that may require additional research in your state's laws or require the assistance of a professional, but it does not use special icons or bold-face warnings to ensure that you don't miss important information.

Quality of Legal Forms   **Grade: B**

The 11 forms and worksheets included with *How to Buy* will assist you in most areas of real estate law that apply to the purchase of a home. The forms are clear and will produce excellent photocopies, but are not perforated for easy removal.

Disclaimer

"This publication is designed to provide accurate and authoritative information in regard to the subject matter covered. It is sold with the understanding that the publisher is not engaged in rendering legal, accounting, or other professional service. If legal advice or other expert assistance is required, the services of a competent professional person should be sought."

Overall   **Grade: B⁺**

At $16.95, ***How to Buy a Condominium or Townhome***
is an excellent resource for anyone in the market to purchase
a home.

Recommended.

How to Negotiate Real Estate Contracts
3rd Edition
by Mark Warda
Sourcebooks, Inc., Naperville, Illinois, 1998
166 pages, $16.95
(800) 226-5291

Good Value

How to Negotiate Real Estate Contracts includes all the essential information you need to understand and negotiate a real estate contract. It also includes an appendix of fill-in-the-blank real estate contract forms for buyers and sellers (a strongly worded contract for the buyer and a neutral one for the seller). Chapters include Preparing Your Contract, When to Use an Attorney, The Buyer's Position, The Seller's Position, The Art of Negotiating, and Federal and Local Laws. A list of basic and recommended clauses is included, as well as information on signing the contract, backing out of the deal, rescuing the deal, and closing.

Accuracy **Grade: A**

Real Estate Contracts provides an accurate, thorough and complete overview of real estate law, and what you need to know before buying or selling real estate. The author is clear at the outset that laws vary from state to state and that some clauses in his book "may not be allowed in certain areas," and that in "some states an approved contract may be required." A chapter is devoted to explaining the federal and local laws that apply to real estate transactions. It covers such issues as lead-based paint, FHA/VA loans, discrimination, and environmental hazards.

Comprehensiveness   **Grade: C⁺**

Real Estate Contracts provides a valuable discussion
of real estate law from both the seller's and buyer's per-
spective. The chapter on federal and local laws is very
helpful, as is the advice in When to Use An Attorney.
However, we found the discussion in the meat of the book
to be somewhat superficial.

Two chapters, Basic Clauses and Recommended
Clauses, comprise half of the book, and include eight
clauses you can find in almost all real estate contracts as
well as 43 optional clauses. Each clause is discussed from
both the seller's and the buyer's points of view. Two or
three options are given for each real estate clause discussed—one that suits the seller, one that suits the buyer
and one that is "neutral."

So far so good. What's missing, at least for the first-
time buyer, is a comprehensive discussion of what each
clause does. Clauses with titles like "conveyance," "in-
gress" and "egress," and "special assessments" come with
little or no explanation. Sometimes you can figure it out
from reading the clause, other times you can't.

The book ends with short (sometimes less than three
full pages) chapters on signing and closing the deal, and
what to do if you need to back out.

Plain Language and Glossary   **Grade: C⁻**

Although ***Real Estate Contracts*** attempts to avoid most
legalese, the text and suggested contract language clauses
are filled with legal and real estate terms that are not always explained. The lack of a glossary is a major
shortcoming of this product.

Easy to Use   **Grade: C⁺**

In general, ***Real Estate Contracts*** is easy to follow and
provides lots of useful information. Step-by-step instructions are not included, however. For someone who has
bought and sold real estate before this may not be a prob-

lem, but it will be one for first-time buyers. To use the forms at the back of the book, you must photocopy and type your information. A form disk, which is not included, would allow you to generate forms more easily and quickly.

Red Flags **Grade: B**
Real Estate Contracts includes fairly extensive warnings about when legal help should be sought, and where state laws may vary, but the warnings are not presented in any obvious way, such as boldface capital lettering, or special icons.

Quality of Legal Forms **Grade: B**
Real Estate Contracts includes forms that can easily be photocopied and completed.

Disclaimer
"This publication is designed to provide accurate and authoritative information in regard to the subject matter covered. It is sold with the understanding that the publisher is not engaged in rendering legal, accounting, or other professional service. If legal advice or other expert assistance is required, the services of a competent professional person should be sought."

Overall **Grade: B⁻**
At $16.95, *Real Estate Contracts* provides a good discussion of real estate law and guidance for experienced buyers and sellers who want to draft their own real estate contracts. For the uninitiated, a publication with more detail, sample clauses, and step-by-step instruction is a better choice.

Good Value.

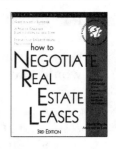

How to Negotiate Real Estate Leases

3rd Edition
by Mark Warda
Sourcebooks, Inc., Naperville, Illinois, 1998
162 pages, $16.95
(800) 226-5291

Good Value

How to Negotiate Real Estate Leases contains all of the essential information you need to understand and negotiate residential or commercial leases from either the landlord or the tenant side. The book explains the different clauses you may find in a lease, discusses which are best for a landlord or tenant, and explains why. It also discusses how to negotiate as either a landlord or tenant, and covers both residential and commercial leases.

Accuracy   **Grade: B**
   Real Estate Leases contains accurate information about leases and the negotiation process.

Comprehensiveness   **Grade: C⁺**
   Real Estate Leases is an informative guide about residential and commercial leases. Every clause you will encounter in a typical lease is explained, and alternatives are provided that favor the landlord or the tenant. These include payment, security deposits, severability, abandonment, access, assignment, pets, maintenance, furnishing, environmental laws, utilities and many more. This product also covers the art of negotiating, federal laws, and the effect of state and local laws. Unfortunately it does not include citations to help you find state laws.

Plain Language and Glossary   **Grade: B**
   Real Estate Leases avoids most legalese, and defines

terminology in the text. It does not include a glossary.

Easy to Use   **Grade: B**

Real Estate Leases is straightforward and easy to use. First, you should read the entire text so you understand the important background information. Then just use the clauses and worksheets as needed while you negotiate your lease.

Red Flags   **Grade: C**

Real Estate Leases points out most areas that may require additional research in your state's laws or require the assistance of a professional, but it does not use special icons or boldface warnings to highlight possible problem areas.

Quality of Legal Forms   **Grade: B**

The 12 sample forms and worksheets provided by *Real Estate Leases* are very helpful and easy to use. The forms are clear and will produce excellent photocopies, but are not perforated for easy removal.

Disclaimer

"This publication is designed to provide accurate and authoritative information in regard to the subject matter covered. It is sold with the understanding that the publisher is not engaged in rendering legal, accounting, or other professional service. If legal advice or other expert assistance is required, the services of a competent professional person should be sought."

Overall   **Grade: B⁻**

At $16.95, *Real Estate Leases* is a good value as a general resource to read before you sign your next residential or commercial lease.

Good Value.

4

TAXES

It has often been said that one of the certainties of life is taxes. Depending on where you live, there are many different kinds of taxes you must pay—sales tax when you buy something, property tax on your house, personal property tax on your car, tax on gasoline, taxes to fly on an airplane, luxury tax and, of course, state and federal income tax. You have no say on most of these taxes. They are simply an added cost to your purchase or a bill that is sent to you.

Income taxes are different though. You are responsible for filing a tax return with the Internal Revenue Service and the tax collecting agency for your state. You tell the government what you earned, what your deductions are, and what you think you owe or should be refunded. Then you wait to see if the government agrees with you. In the past, you could either fill out your own tax returns or hire a professional accountant or lawyer to do it for you.

Until recently, to do it yourself meant sitting down with the tax forms, all of the instructions and IRS notices, your receipts, your W-2's and 1099's and going line by line through the confusing forms. The only real help you could get was from thick tax guides that were nearly as difficult to understand as IRS forms. These aids helped you fill out your return correctly, but did not save time, and even added to your confusion.

We all know how much time it can take to fill out your tax returns, including the frustration of dealing with a tax code that no one seems to understand. If you chose to hire a professional, you saved yourself the headache of doing your tax return in exchange for paying hundreds and even thousands of dollars in preparation fees.

For most people, who do not have extremely complicated tax returns, there is now a better way to do it yourself, save time and avoid frustration. Software developers for home computers realized that much of the filing process can be automated to save time and provide better accuracy (no math mistakes). The first programs were designed for accountants and were often very complex. Eventually though, the complexities were hidden behind very sophisticated user interfaces that ask a series of questions, and automatically complete your tax return.

Tax preparation software has quickly become a cheap and easy way to file your tax returns. These programs have grown beyond just filling out your returns; they now offer detailed information on the tax code, multimedia help and advice by tax experts, planning tips for next year's returns, and even allow you to file your tax returns electronically with the IRS.

The products reviewed in this chapter include the two primary software programs used by consumers to complete their federal and state income tax returns. We also briefly look at reference books that can provide help for consumers who do not have access to a computer.

Of these tools, we believe Intuit's *TurboTax Deluxe* is an extraordinary product that truly defines the state-of-the-art for do-it-yourselfers who have access to a personal computer. It is a HALT Do-it-Yourself Best Buy.

TurboTax Deluxe

Intuit, Tucson, Arizona,
new version every year
CD-ROM Software for Windows 3.1/95, also available as
Quicken MacInTax Deluxe for Mac, $39.95
TurboTax State Modules, $27.95
(800) 922-3538

HALT
Do-it-Yourself
Best Buy

TurboTax Deluxe bills itself as easy, fast and complete, and, especially when compared to doing it with pen and paper, it is. *TurboTax* contains virtually every tax form and worksheet that you're likely to need when preparing your federal tax returns. It provides a well-organized process for completing your return and filing it with the Internal Revenue Service. The program also provides instant access to official IRS publications, multimedia video clips of tax experts, Money Magazine's *Income Tax Handbook* and Jeff Schnepper's *How to Pay Zero Taxes*. Also included is a user's guide and QuickStart Card.

Accuracy   **Grade: A**
> *TurboTax* provides thorough, accurate and up-to-date information including the latest changes to the tax code. If other tax code changes are made for that tax year, updates are easily downloaded from the Intuit web site.

Comprehensiveness   **Grade: A**
> *TurboTax* is a very thorough product that features every form and worksheet you're likely to need, as well as a comprehensive tax library of IRS publications, popular reference books, and video clips by tax experts Marshall Loeb and Mary Sprouse. *TurboTax* also includes a section that answers over 200 frequently asked tax questions,

and a tax planner for those who want to plan ahead for the next tax year.

For your state taxes, Intuit offers a separate program called *TurboTax State* that imports the information it needs from *TurboTax* and asks any additional questions that your state return requires. With both of these products, your state and federal tax returns may be completed quickly and efficiently.

Plain Language and Glossary   **Grade: A**

TurboTax uses plain language throughout, and clearly defines tax terminology. It also contains an extensive help system that includes detailed definitions and explanations of tax terminology.

Easy to Use   **Grade: A**

TurboTax is very easy to install using a standard setup utility. The actual program has a well-polished interface that is easy to use and intuitive. A tabbed window takes you through the process of filling out and filing your tax return in a step-by-step fashion. You can move between sections, though it is best to go in order. At any time you can access the tax library to answer questions you may have about taxes or the user's guide to answer questions about how to do something in the program.

First, there is the Start tab. Here you input your personal information. Second, is the Import tab which allows you to import financial data from personal finance programs like *Quicken* or *QuickBooks*. If you use a financial program, you can save a lot of time by using this step. Third, is the Interview. This is the most important section and consists of a long series of questions which, as you answer, will fill out your tax return, associated worksheets and schedules.

During this process, you have access to the extensive tax library, the video tax advisor, IRS publications and other references. With especially tricky areas, *TurboTax* uses a Guide Me feature that presents a set of more detailed questions to gather information for your return. After each question is completed you click a Next button to progress, though you may also click a Back button if you wish to go back to change or review a previous answer.

Fourth, is the Review. Here, *TurboTax* examines your return by checking for errors, deductions you missed, and entries that may trigger an audit. It will also compare your return to U.S. averages and suggest ways to reduce your future taxes. Fifth, is the State section where, in conjunction with *TurboTax State* (sold separately), you can complete your state tax returns. Sixth, is Filing. At this point you may print your return to send to the IRS or you may file it electronically through Intuit. Finally, there is Planning. This section allows you to plan for the next tax year.

If you are a tax whiz, and do not require the interview process, *TurboTax* also allows you to choose the forms you need and fill them out directly.

Red Flags   **Grade: A**

TurboTax automatically keeps you aware of possible trouble areas as you complete the interview through warning boxes that appear between questions. *TurboTax* also checks your return for errors and possible entries that may trigger an audit by the IRS.

Quality of Legal Forms   **Grade: A⁺**

TurboTax contains almost every form or worksheet that you're likely to need to file your return, including the 1040PC (a special form that omits lines you did not use). The forms are clear, and look exactly like those supplied by the IRS.

Disclaimer

"Tax laws and regulations change frequently and their application can vary widely based upon the specific facts and circumstances involved. Users are encouraged to consult with their own professional tax advisors concerning their specific tax circumstances. Intuit disclaims any responsibility for the accuracy or adequacy of any positions taken by users in their tax returns."

Overall   **Grade: A**

For $39.95 ***TurboTax*** or ***MacInTax*** are exceptional values, and allow almost anyone to quickly and easily prepare and file their tax returns. At $27.95, ***TurboTax State*** is also an exceptional value that allows consumers to seamlessly complete both federal and state income tax returns in a simple session on a home computer. The ***TurboTax*** line of products truly defines the state-of-the-art in do-it-yourself products.

HALT
Do-it-Yourself
Best Buy

Kiplinger TaxCut Deluxe

Federal Filing Edition
Block Financial Corporation, Kansas City, Missouri,
new version every year
CD-ROM for Windows 3.1/95, and Mac, $29.95
TaxCut MultiState CD-ROM, $24.95
(800) 818-7940

Recommended

Kiplinger TaxCut Deluxe provides users with a fast and easy way to complete their federal tax returns. ***TaxCut*** contains more than 100 different tax forms and worksheets, which cover the areas that most people need. The software also provides tax tips, the full IRS instructions for tax forms, and detailed explanations of each form. Also included is a Quick Start guide to the software.

Accuracy   **Grade: A**
   TaxCut provides accurate and up-to-date information, including the latest changes to the tax code. If other tax code changes are made for that tax year, updates are easily downloaded from the **TaxCut** web site.

Comprehensiveness   **Grade: B**
   TaxCut is a thorough product that provides you with all of the forms and information you need to file your own federal tax return. ***TaxCut*** features an extensive help system that includes *Kiplinger's Tax Tips*, IRS instructions for tax forms, detailed explanations of every tax form, and audio and video tax advice. If the program does not include a form you need, it will tell you which tax form you need by its number. Lacking in ***TaxCut*** are the nice extras included with its competition, *TurboTax*, such as Money Magazine's *Income Tax Handbook*, and Jeff Schnepper's *How to Pay Zero Taxes*. Although not man-

datory, these extras are very helpful and add a little more polish to the competition.

For your state taxes, *TaxCut* also comes in state editions that import information from your *TaxCut* return. However, the *TaxCut MultiState* CD-ROM only includes 24 states for Windows and five for the Mac, which is obviously of no help if you live in a state not covered by the product.

Plain Language and Glossary   **Grade: A**
TaxCut uses plain English and defines any tax terminology through the thorough help system that serves as an interactive glossary.

Easy to Use   **Grade: A**
TaxCut is very easy to install using a standard setup utility. The program has an extremely well-polished interface that is easy to use and intuitive. A window, where each of the numbered tabs is a step in the process, helps you prepare your tax return. You just click on a tab to move to that step, and when you're done, the program will move you to the next step.

First, there is the Quick Start tab. Here you create a new file, and have the option of importing your financial information from a financial program like *Quicken*, or *Microsoft Money*. If you use a financial program, you can save a lot of time by using this step.

Second, is Q & A. This is the most important section and consists of a long series of questions which, as you answer, complete your tax return, associated worksheets and schedules. At all times you have access to the extensive tax library, and often audio or video tax advice will appear. With especially tricky questions, *TaxCut* provides a subset of detailed questions that gather the information required for your return. After each question is completed you click a Next button to move forward. You may also click a

Back button to change or review a previous answer.

Third is the Forms tab. If you know what you're doing, you can access forms directly and fill them out. This step is skipped when you do the normal step-by-step Q & A method.

Fourth is the Auditor, which checks your tax return for missing information, inconsistencies and entries that may trigger an IRS audit.

Fifth is the Review tab. Here *TaxCut* allows you to view summaries of your tax return that include the important numbers from your return, charts showing where your taxable income went and a list of your entries.

Sixth, there is the State section where, in conjunction with *TaxCut MultiState* CD-ROM (sold separately), you can complete your state tax returns. Seventh, is Print & File. At this point you may print your return to send to the IRS or you may file it electronically. Finally, there is Next Year. This section presents tax planning advice for the next tax year.

You can move between sections, although it is best to go in order. At any time, you can access the help section which contains tax information to answer questions about taxes, or the program guide to answer questions about how to use the program.

Red Flags **Grade: A**

TaxCut automatically keeps you aware of possible trouble areas as you complete the interview through warning boxes that appear between questions. *TaxCut* also checks your return for errors and possible entries that may trigger an audit by the IRS.

Quality of Legal Forms **Grade: A⁻**

TaxCut contains almost every form or worksheet that you're likely to need to file your return including the 1040PC (a special form that omits lines you did not use). The forms are clear and look exactly like those supplied by the IRS. As previously noted, this product does not, however, cover all states.

Disclaimer
None.

Overall   **Grade: B⁺**
For $29.95, *TaxCut* is an excellent value for doing your own yearly federal tax returns without hiring a professional tax return preparer. At $24.95, **TaxCut MultiState** is also an excellent product, but only for the 24 states it covers for Windows users and the five states for Mac users.

Recommended.

Recommended Reading

J.K. Lasser's Your Income Tax, 1999
Macmillan Publishing Company, 1999. 758 pages. $14.95

Lasser's is the standard, comprehensive reference guide that has everything you need to prepare and file your taxes. In a user-friendly format, **Your Income Tax** includes expert tax advice, practical examples, money-saving tips, tax planning strategies, illustrated forms, and special tax planning sections for the self-employed, investors, senior citizens, homeowners and families.

The Ernst & Young Tax Saver's Guide, 1999
John Wiley & Sons, Inc., 1999, 302 pages. $12.95

The **Tax Saver's Guide** offers hundreds of ideas and unique, money-saving tax tips that make it easy to save on your income taxes. It also includes everything you need to know about changes to the tax law, and explains how to meet any new requirements for deductions and exemptions.

5

BANKRUPTCY

Each year growing numbers of American consumers take advantage of the bankruptcy laws to liquidate or reorganize their debts. With the explosion of easy credit in recent years, this trend has continued and is accelerating.

As the *Washington Post* reported on Sunday June 7, 1998, well over one million households filed for bankruptcy protection in 1997 (p. 1):

> Despite a booming economy, the number of personal bankruptcy filings keeps escalating, hitting record numbers last year for the third consecutive year and again in the first quarter of this year.
>
> From 1996 to 1997, filings jumped 20 percent to 1.35 million, or one in every 70 households.

Because consumers who seek bankruptcy protection are in financial distress, do-it-yourself kits, publications and software are particularly appealing. Ironically, hiring a lawyer may actually be more economical for some people who file for bankruptcy, because legal fees are taken off the top when a consumer's assets are liquidated to satisfy creditors, so there is sometimes little or no net cost for legal services. For others, an additional bill of any kind is the last thing they need. Under any circumstances, however, the consumer is going to have to complete much of the legwork to catalog assets and compile a comprehensive list of creditors, so self-help materials are extremely valuable.

You should keep in mind that there are two basic forms of bankruptcy protection—"debt liquidation" under Chapter 7 of the bankruptcy code, where creditors accept a partial payment and your debts are extinguished, and "debt reorganization" under Chapter 13 of the bankruptcy code, where creditors accept a schedule for you to repay all the money owed.

Corporations, partnerships and other businesses can also secure protection under Chapter 11 of the bankruptcy code, and there are special provisions that allow family farmers to reorganize their debts under Chapter 12. Consumers can only liquidate their debts under Chapter 7 once every ten years, but they can reorganize debts more frequently.

Deciding which approach, if any, is right for you is one of the most important decisions in the bankruptcy process, and the information provided about these differing approaches in self-help materials weighs heavily in our evaluation. While bankruptcy is a right that protects you from being hounded by your creditors, it can have a substantial impact on your future ability to secure credit and to manage your financial affairs. We therefore also considered the information about alternatives to bankruptcy provided by self-help materials as a critical factor in evaluating them.

Like other specialized areas of the law, there is a special vocabulary that the bankruptcy courts have developed. In addition to our usual emphasis on plain language and avoiding legalese, we gave extra weight to self-help materials that include complete glossaries and appendices to explain legal terminology.

Finally, the bankruptcy courts have long used standardized forms. Because so much of the bankruptcy process is simply filing accurate and complete paperwork, we gave special consideration to self-help materials that include preliminary worksheets and step-by-step instructions for completing forms, and that produce easy-to-read final forms.

How to File for Bankruptcy from Nolo Press stands out as the best comprehensive resource for do-it-yourself consumers who need bankruptcy protection and is a HALT Do-it-Yourself Best Buy. There are also exceptional values in other products that are tailored to meet the needs of people who already know which approach–Chapter 7 or Chapter 13–is better for their situation.

How to File for Bankruptcy
7th Edition
by Stephen Elias, Albin Renauer & Robin Leonard
Nolo Press, Berkeley, California, 1998
475 pages, $26.95
(800) 992-6656

HALT
Do-it-Yourself
Best Buy

How to File for Bankruptcy offers a complete overview, step-by-step instructions and the latest forms for filing a Chapter 7 (liquidation of debts) bankruptcy. It also includes a brief explanation of other bankruptcy proceedings (Chapters 11, 12 and, in slightly more detail, Chapter 13) to help readers decide if Chapter 7 is indeed the way to go. *How to File* also offers advice for married couples and a "fast-track" icon that allows readers to skip material not pertinent to their situation. The appendices include state and federal exemption tables, a glossary, addresses of bankruptcy courts, and bankruptcy forms.

Accuracy   **Grade: A**
> *How to File* provides an extremely thorough and accurate discussion of the laws governing Chapter 7 bankruptcy. The 7th Edition includes supplemental sheets with the latest changes in the bankruptcy code and updated forms. Nolo's web site also provides additional bankruptcy updates.

Comprehensiveness   **Grade: A⁺**
> The authors leave no stone unturned. In addition to explaining Chapter 7, bankruptcy forms, and the court process, *How to File* includes tons of follow-up information including a Life After Bankruptcy chapter that explains what you can expect from creditors and various ways to

get back on your financial feet. Information on getting help, including using nonlawyer bankruptcy petition preparers, online resources, law library resources or help from a lawyer, are also discussed in detail.

Plain Language and Glossary   **Grade: A⁻**
Legalese is used only when unavoidable and is always explained in the text. ***How to File*** includes a glossary of "exemption" terms. The lack of a more extensive glossary is one gap that could be filled in future editions.

Easy to Use   **Grade: A⁻**
How to File is extremely easy to use and understand. Fictional examples are sprinkled throughout to help illustrate points made in the text, sample bankruptcy forms are explained clause-by-clause, and step-by-step instructions are included on how to complete and file the forms. A big improvement would be including bankruptcy forms on disk for computer users.

Red Flags   **Grade: A⁺**
Special icons flag areas that warrant special attention. ***How to File*** explains when local rules may vary, when consumers need to contact a lawyer and when other resources should be consulted. Potential pitfalls are also highlighted to help consumers avoid inaccurate or incomplete reporting.

Quality of Legal Forms   **Grade: A**
How to File includes worksheets, a sample letter to the bankruptcy court asking about local requirements and filing fee costs, and all of the official forms you need to file a Chapter 7 Bankruptcy. The forms are easy to read, complete and reproduce.

Disclaimer

"We've done our best to give you useful and accurate information in this book. But laws and procedures change frequently and are subject to differing interpretations. If you want legal advice backed by a guarantee, see a lawyer. If you use this book, it's your responsibility to make sure that the facts and general advice contained in it are applicable to your situation."

Overall   **Grade: A**

How to File for Bankruptcy is well-written, easy to understand and thorough. The only improvements we can suggest are a more complete glossary and a form disk. Readers will come away with a good understanding of Chapter 7 bankruptcy law, their rights and responsibilities under it, and a realistic notion of what's involved before, during and after the proceeding. At $26.95, *How to File for Bankruptcy* is an exceptional value for anyone who is considering bankruptcy, and a comprehensive resource for do-it-yourself consumers.

HALT
Do-it-Yourself
Best Buy

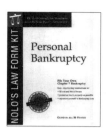

Nolo's Law Form Kit: Personal Bankruptcy

Steve Elias, Albin Renauer, Robin Leonard
and Lisa Goldoftas
Nolo Press, Berkeley, California, 1997
169 pages, and 1998 update supplement, $14.95
(800) 992-6656

Recommended

Personal Bankruptcy was created for people who wish to file
a simple Chapter 7 bankruptcy in common situations. It contains a general overview and description of the bankruptcy
system, and the legal forms required to file in federal bankruptcy court. The book's primary focus is on Chapter 7 (debt
liquidations), but it also provides general information on Chapter 11 (debt reorganizations for businesses) and Chapter 13
(debt reorganization for individuals). If you have a simple and
straightforward Chapter 7 bankruptcy, this book has what you
need. **Personal Bankruptcy** contains a detailed state-by-state
listing of property exempt from bankruptcy, and all the schedules and legal forms (with detailed instructions and thorough
examples) required to file for Chapter 7 proceedings.

Accuracy   **Grade: B⁺**

    Personal Bankruptcy provides accurate and fairly de-
tailed information on Chapter 7 bankruptcy. It does not
include specific details of bankruptcy law, and recommends that the reader should see a lawyer if they have
complex bankruptcy needs or refer to **How to File for
Bankruptcy.**

Comprehensiveness   **Grade: B⁺**

    The title claims that **Personal Bankruptcy** is for filing
your own Chapter 7 bankruptcy, and that is what this book

provides for simple and commonplace situations. This is adequate for most individuals, and *Personal Bankruptcy* does tell you where to find detailed information for more complex situations, and when you need to consult an attorney.

Plain Language and Glossary   **Grade: B**
Personal Bankruptcy avoids almost all legalese and defines bankruptcy terminology in the text. The lack of a glossary that explains legal terminology is a major shortcoming of this product, particularly since the book is geared toward do-it-yourself consumers who will have to deal with bankruptcy terminology on their own.

Easy to Use   **Grade: A**
Personal Bankruptcy is well-organized and takes you through a Chapter 7 filing in a step-by-step fashion. It reviews each form and schedule you must use, provides an example to follow, and explains each field you must complete. This ensures that you understand each and every part of the bankruptcy forms, and avoids confusion. The book also provides information for troublesome areas like retirement plans and married couples, and cautions the reader in areas that might pose potential problems in filing.

Red Flags   **Grade: A**
Personal Bankruptcy contains a very thorough appendix of state-by-state property exemptions and citations to applicable state statutes. Helpful tips throughout the text provide information on special rules and other warnings.

Quality of Legal Forms   **Grade: A**
Personal Bankruptcy provides all of the forms and schedules necessary in filing Chapter 7 bankruptcy, tells you how to photocopy them to regulation size, and provides thorough explanations and examples for each form

and schedule. Forms are very legible, are perforated for easy removal, and will produce excellent photocopies.

Disclaimer

"We've done our best to give you useful and accurate information in this kit. But this kit does not take the place of a lawyer licensed to practice law in your state. If you want legal advice backed by a guarantee, see a lawyer. If you use any information contained in this kit, it's your personal responsibility to make sure that the facts and general information in it are applicable to your situation."

Overall **Grade: B⁺**

For the do-it-yourselfer who wants to file a Chapter 7 bankruptcy that is not complex, *Personal Bankruptcy* is an excellent kit that will provide all the necessary forms and walk you through the process. If you have a more complex bankruptcy, or would like to know about the legal issues that surround bankruptcy, *How to File for Bankruptcy* is a detailed do-it-yourself Chapter 7 bankruptcy book (see previous review). At $14.95, *Nolo's Law Form Kit: Personal Bankruptcy* is an exceptional value.

Recommended.

Chapter 13 Bankruptcy:
Repay Your Debts
3rd Edition
by Robin Leonard
Nolo Press, Berkeley, California, 1998   **Recommended**
368 pages, $29.95
(800) 992-6656

Chapter 13 Bankruptcy: Repay Your Debts provides an
overview of the bankruptcy process, and general discussions of
procedures for individuals under Chapter 13 (reorganization of
debts by individuals). It does provide a brief discussion of
proceedings under Chapter 7 (liquidation of debts), but this
book does not discuss Chapter 11 (reorganization of debts by
businesses) or Chapter 12 (reorganization for family farmers)
proceedings. *Chapter 13 Bankruptcy* also provides a detailed state-by-state listing of property exemptions from bankruptcy, the addresses of bankruptcy courts, eight worksheets,
and 25 legal forms for individual debt reorganization proceedings.

Accuracy   **Grade: B**
   Chapter 13 Bankruptcy includes an accurate and fairly
   detailed discussion of individual debt reorganization under Chapter 13. It does not include many details of
   bankruptcy law and procedures for consumers with more
   complex financial needs.

Comprehensiveness   **Grade: B⁺**
   Chapter 13 Bankruptcy provides detailed information
   about individual debt reorganization under Chapter 13,
   but provides only cursory information about individual
   debt liquidation, and does not discuss business and family

farmer bankruptcy. Some discussion of these other bankruptcy procedures would be helpful, so you can have some
confidence that you are using the right approach to your
financial problems. The book is also shipped with update
sheets that provide information on recent changes in the
law, and is supplemented by information posted on the
Nolo Press Internet site.

Plain Language and Glossary **Grade: B**
Chapter 13 Bankruptcy successfully avoids almost all
legalese, and explains most important bankruptcy terminology in the text. The lack of a glossary that explains
legal terminology is a major shortcoming for this product,
particularly since the book is geared toward do-it-yourself
consumers who will have to deal with bankruptcy terminology on their own.

Easy to Use **Grade: A⁻**
Chapter 13 Bankruptcy keeps its explanations at a basic
level, but provides a wealth of detail about bankruptcy
proceedings. Its step-by-step instructions and worksheets
make the book especially attractive for do-it-yourself consumers. Finally, the use of special "fast track" icons helps
to quickly guide consumers to essential information.

Red Flags **Grade: A**
Chapter 13 Bankruptcy includes an exceptionally detailed appendix of state-by-state property exemptions and
citations to applicable state statutes. Special icons are used
to alert consumers to potential problems, to situations
where they will need legal advice from a lawyer, and to
other resources.

Quality of Legal Forms **Grade: B⁺**
Chapter 13 Bankruptcy includes eight worksheets and
25 legal forms for Chapter 13 proceedings. They are

legible, easy to read and produce high quality photocopies. The step-by-step instructions in this product should help consumers produce completed documents that are accepted by court clerks.

Disclaimer

"We've done our best to give you useful and accurate information in this book. But laws and procedures change frequently and are subject to differing interpretations. If you want legal advice backed by a guarantee, see a lawyer. If you use this book, it's your responsibility to make sure that the facts and general advice contained in it are applicable to your situation."

Overall   **Grade: B⁺**

For consumers who decide that a debt reorganization is their best course, ***Chapter 13 Bankruptcy: Repay Your Debts*** provides a good guide. The lack of glossary is its one shortcoming. For do-it-yourselfers who need to file a simple, routine bankruptcy, and who have other references to guide them, at $29.95, ***Chapter 13 Bankruptcy*** is an excellent value.

Recommended.

Debt Free:
The National Bankruptcy Kit
1st Edition
by Daniel Sitarz
Nova Publishing, Carbondale, Illinois, 1995
255 pages, $17.95
(800) 748-1175

Recommended

Debt Free: The National Bankruptcy Kit provides a
general overview of Chapter 7 bankruptcy law (liquidation of
debts), worksheets for gathering information, step-by-step instructions, and the official forms needed to file a Chapter 7
bankruptcy. It also includes a brief explanation of other bankruptcy proceedings (Chapters 11, 12 and 13) and a list of
reasons why Chapter 7 may not be the right choice for you. The
appendices include bankruptcy forms, state and federal exemption tables, and addresses of federal bankruptcy courts.

Accuracy   **Grade: B⁻**
   Debt Free gives an accurate, but abbreviated, discussion
   of the laws governing Chapter 7 bankruptcy. Only 12
   pages are devoted to the topic and the discussion is very
   general. The latest changes in bankruptcy law are not re-
   flected in the appropriate forms.

Comprehensiveness   **Grade: B**
   The author's stated intention is to give the reader a "basic
   understanding of bankruptcy." While ***Debt Free*** lacks
   detail, it does provide a good selection of worksheets, check
   lists, step-by-step instructions and state-specific appendices.

Plain Language and Glossary   **Grade: A**
   The book is written in plain language. Legal terms are
used only when necessary, shown in italics and defined
when first used. ***Debt Free*** also includes an extensive
plain language glossary of legal terms.

Easy to Use   **Grade: B⁺**
Debt Free is easy to understand and use. Chapter 4,
Filling Out the Official Bankruptcy Forms, is a hefty chapter that completes each form by way of example, and
explains it clause by clause. This kind of meticulous pre-
sentation of "how to do it," accompanied by state-specific
laws in the back of the book, makes the publication very
user-friendly. A major improvement would be including
bankruptcy forms on disk for computer users.

Red Flags   **Grade: C**
   Some warnings are included about when expert legal help
should be sought or when you should be particularly careful, but they are not highlighted in any obvious way such
as boldface, capital lettering or special icons.

Quality of Legal Forms   **Grade: A**
Debt Free includes worksheets and all the official forms
you need to file a Chapter 7 bankruptcy. The forms can
easily be photocopied and used by do-it-yourselfers.

Disclaimer
   "This publication is designed to provide accurate and authoritative information in regard to the subject matter
covered. It is sold with the understanding that the publisher and author are not engaged in rendering legal,
accounting, or other professional services. If legal advice
or other expert assistance is required, the services of a
competent professional person should be sought."

Overall **Grade: B⁺**

Consumers can get a quick feel for bankruptcy proceedings, and have on hand all the forms they need. They should not rely solely on this product, however, if doing it themselves. At $17.95, *Debt Free: The National Bankruptcy Kit* is an excellent value.

Recommended.

Bankruptcy Step-by-Step
by James John Jurinski
Barron's Educational Series, Inc.
Hauppauge, New York, 1996
225 pages, $14.95
(800) 645-3476

Good Value

Bankruptcy Step-by-Step is designed to provide individuals with the information to file their own bankruptcy. It contains a general overview and description of the bankruptcy system and the legal forms required to file in federal bankruptcy court. The book's primary focus is on Chapter 7 (liquidations), but it also provides some information on Chapter 11 (reorganization of debts by business) and Chapter 13 (reorganization of debts by individuals). ***Bankruptcy Step-by-Step*** contains a detailed state-by-state listing of property exempt from bankruptcy, the addresses and phone numbers of bankruptcy courts, inventory and debt worksheets, and the necessary worksheets and legal forms required to file for Chapter 7 proceedings.

Accuracy   **Grade: B⁻**
   Bankruptcy Step-by-Step provides accurate and fairly detailed information on Chapter 7 liquidation. It does not include specific details of bankruptcy law and recommends that the reader should see a lawyer if they have complex bankruptcy needs. 1998 updates are not included.

Comprehensiveness   **Grade: C**
   Although the title says "Bankruptcy," the book focuses primarily on Chapter 7 with some additional information on Chapters 11 and 13, and only a cursory mention of Chapters 9 and 12. Although adequate for most individuals,

Bankruptcy Step-by-Step would be a poor choice for a small business. It does, however, contain the information necessary to file a Chapter 7 bankruptcy yourself or work more knowledgeably with an attorney.

Plain Language and Glossary **Grade: A**
Bankruptcy Step-by-Step avoids almost all legalese and provides an excellent glossary of bankruptcy terminology.

Easy to Use **Grade: B⁺**
Bankruptcy Step-by-Step is well organized and takes you through a Chapter 7 filing in a step-by-step fashion. Each chapter ends with a question and answer section that summarizes the material contained in the chapter in a concise format. The hints and examples for completing the required forms will aid most consumers who are filing a straightforward Chapter 7 liquidation.

Red Flags **Grade: A**
Bankruptcy Step-by-Step contains a thorough appendix of state-by-state property exemptions and citations to applicable state statutes. Helpful planning tips are placed throughout the text to answer frequently asked questions and provide warnings. An entire chapter is devoted to possible problems to anticipate including liens, taxes, and special exemptions.

Quality of Legal Forms **Grade: A⁻**
Bankruptcy Step-by-Step provides all of the forms and schedules necessary in filing a Chapter 7 bankruptcy. It also contains hints and examples for completing the forms. Forms are very legible, are perforated for easy removal, and will produce excellent copies.

Disclaimer

"Although the material in this book concerns legal issues, the answers you find here should not be regarded as legal advice and should not be substituted for legal advice. The discussions in the text are of necessity generalized, and a slight change in fact or local law may change an answer. Additionally, although every effort has been made at the time of this writing to ensure that this material is accurate, law is constantly changing as statutes are passed and cases decided. If you have a question concerning a material matter, it would be wise to seek legal advice from a competent attorney in your community."

Overall   **Grade: B**

For the do-it-yourselfer who wants to file a Chapter 7 bankruptcy that is not complex, at $14.95 ***Bankruptcy Step-by-Step*** is a good reference manual that will provide the necessary forms and walk you through the process.

Good Value.

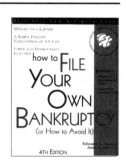

How to File Your Own Bankruptcy (Or How to Avoid It)

4th Edition
by Edward A. Haman
Sourcebooks, Inc., Naperville, Illinois, 1998
200 pages, $19.95
(800) 226-5291

Good Value

How to File Your Own Bankruptcy (Or How to Avoid It)
provides a general overview of the bankruptcy process, and
general discussions of procedures for individuals under Chapter 7 (liquidation) and Chapter 13 (reorganization). It does not
discuss proceedings under Chapter 11 (reorganization by businesses) or Chapter 12 (reorganization for family farmers). *How
to File* also provides a detailed state-by-state listing of property
exempt from bankruptcy, three worksheets and 25 legal forms
for Chapter 7 and Chapter 13 proceedings.

Accuracy   **Grade: C⁺**
How to File provides an accurate but "bare-bones" discussion of individual debt liquidation under Chapter 7 and
individual debt reorganization under Chapter 13. It does
not include many details of bankruptcy law and procedures
for consumers with more complex financial needs.

Comprehensiveness   **Grade: C**
How to File is limited to very basic information about
bankruptcy, and does not discuss business or family farmer
bankruptcy. Some discussion of these other bankruptcy
procedures would be helpful to consumers, so they can
have some confidence that they are using the right approach
to their debt problems.

Plain Language and Glossary   **Grade: C**
How to File successfully avoids almost all legalese, in
part because it is somewhat superficial. The lack of a glossary that explains legal terminology is a major shortcoming
in this product, particularly since the book is geared toward do-it-yourself consumers who will have to deal with
bankruptcy terminology on their own.

Easy to Use   **Grade: B**
How to File keeps its explanations at the very basic level
and is therefore limited, but its step-by-step instructions
and worksheets make the book especially attractive for do-
it-yourself consumers.

Red Flags   **Grade: A**
How to File includes an exceptionally detailed appendix
of state-by-state property exemptions and citations to applicable state statutes. Special Warning and Caution boxes
are also included in the text, telling consumers about problems they can avoid.

Quality of Legal Forms   **Grade: B**
How to File includes three worksheets and 25 legal forms
for Chapter 7 and Chapter 13 proceedings. They are legible, easy to read and produce high-quality photocopies.
The step-by-step instructions in *How to File* should help
consumers produce completed forms that are accepted by
court clerks. Only the basic bankruptcy forms are included, however.

Disclaimer
"This publication is designed to provide accurate and authoritative information in regard to the subject matter
covered. It is sold with the understanding that the publisher is not engaged in rendering legal, accounting or other
professional service. If legal advice or other expert assis-

tance is required, the services of a competent professional person should be sought."

Overall **Grade: C⁺**

The lack of a glossary and its limited coverage means that ***How to File Your Own Bankruptcy*** is probably not the best book for all do-it-yourself consumers. At $19.95 ***How to File Your Own Bankruptcy*** is a good buy for consumers who need to file a simple, routine bankruptcy, and who have other references to guide them through the legalese that courts still use.

Good Value.

The Bankruptcy Kit

2nd Edition
by John Ventura
Dearborn Financial Publishing, Chicago, Illinois, 1996
214 pages, $19.95
(312) 836-4400

Good Value

The Bankruptcy Kit provides general background information on the bankruptcy process, as well as fairly detailed discussions of procedures for individuals under Chapter 7 (liquidation) and Chapter 13 (reorganization). It does not discuss proceedings under Chapter 11 (reorganization by businesses) or Chapter 12 (reorganization for family farmers). It also provides a nationwide index of bankruptcy trustees, and state-by-state listing of property exempt from bankruptcy. Although ***The Bankruptcy Kit*** includes basic forms for consumers seeking protection under Chapter 7 and Chapter 13, this publication is designed to be used in conjunction with the professional services of a lawyer.

Accuracy **Grade: C+**

The Bankruptcy Kit's discussion of individual debt liquidation under Chapter 7 and individual debt reorganization under Chapter 13 provides basic, accurate information about bankruptcy law, but does not provide some of the more detailed information that you are expected to obtain from a lawyer.

Comprehensiveness **Grade: C**

The Bankruptcy Kit limits itself to basic information and does not discuss business and family farmer bankruptcy in any useful way. Some discussion of these other bankruptcy procedures would be helpful to consumers, so they can have some confidence that they are using the right approach to their debt problems.

Plain Language and Glossary   **Grade: C**
While *The Bankruptcy Kit* makes a valiant effort to avoid legalese, it does sometimes lapse into rather dense legal terminology. If the book is purchased to help understand the bankruptcy process and deal more knowledgeably with a lawyer, this is not a major drawback. But for a do-it-yourself consumer, this is not the most accessible publication. The three page glossary provides accurate and accessible definitions, but does not cover all the legal terms used in the text. It would be helpful to have a more extensive glossary, so readers don't have to search through the book to find the meaning of a term they have forgotten. *The Bankruptcy Kit* also includes a separate appendix that explains motions and objections used in Bankruptcy Court.

Easy to Use   **Grade: C⁻**
The Bankruptcy Kit sometimes suffers from a confused organization—using terminology and concepts to describe the bankruptcy process before they are fully explained to the consumer. The lack of step-by-step instructions and checklists also make the book less attractive, particularly for do-it-yourself consumers.

Red Flags   **Grade: A**
The Bankruptcy Kit includes a detailed appendix of state-by-state property exemptions and applicable state statutes. Special "Warning" boxes are also included in the text, telling consumers what questions to ask their lawyer, and alerting them to some of the common mistakes made by people in serious financial trouble.

Quality of Legal Forms   **Grade: D**
In keeping with ***The Bankruptcy Kit's*** design as a guide to
be used in conjunction with the professional services of
a lawyer, the appendices of legal forms are better suited
for background information than for actual use by consumers. Reproduced in an extremely small typeface (we
estimate either 6pt or 8pt), it is doubtful that legible photocopies can be produced and completed for do-it-yourself
use. The forms are also difficult to read.

Disclaimer
"This publication is designed to provide accurate and authoritative information in regard to the subject matter
covered. It is sold with the understanding that the publisher is not engaged in rendering legal, accounting or other
professional service. If legal advice or other expert assistance is required, the services of a competent professional
person should be sought."

Overall   **Grade: C**
The lack of usable self-help forms and the simplistic nature of ***The Bankruptcy Kit*** means it's probably not the
book for do-it-yourself consumers. At $19.95, the ***Kit*** does
provide good value for basic information that will help consumers who hire a lawyer for bankruptcy.

                                        Good Value.

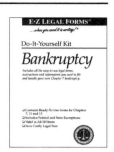

Do-It-Yourself Kit: Bankruptcy

E-Z Legal Forms, Inc., Deerfield Beach, Florida, 1991
Form Kit, $21.95
(954) 480-8933

Not Recommended

Do-It-Yourself Kit: Bankruptcy includes a small information pamphlet and the forms needed to file a Chapter 7, 11 or 13 Bankruptcy. Federal and state property exemption laws and a glossary of terms are included. Consumers are encouraged to have their forms reviewed, or to work with an attorney from the outset, if there is anything about the product they do not understand (including its "adequacy to protect"), or if they plan to file for bankruptcy protection under Chapter 11 or 13.

Accuracy   **Grade: C**
The ***Do-It-Yourself Kit*** gives an accurate but cursory discussion of the laws governing bankruptcy. The forms, which comply with the Bankruptcy Reform Act of 1994, do not include some of the most recent changes in bankruptcy law.

Comprehensiveness   **Grade: C**
While the ***Do-It-Yourself Kit*** provides all the forms you need for Chapters 7, 11 and 13, information about your rights and responsibilities under each of these proceedings is scant. The pamphlet focuses on Chapter 7 and advises consumers to discuss their options "with an experienced bankruptcy attorney" before filing papers on their own.

Plain Language and Glossary   **Grade: D**

Although written primarily in plain-language, the ***Do-It-Yourself Kit*** uses legal terms and concepts but doesn't define them. This product does contain a small two-page glossary of terms, but many important bankruptcy terms are not defined in it.

Easy to Use   **Grade: D**

The ***Do-It-Yourself Kit*** briefly explains each form and when it should be used. However, the lack of detailed step-by-step instructions for completing the forms, or sample completed forms, makes this product less useful to the true do-it-yourselfer.

Red Flags   **Grade: B‑**

A special section called "Errors to Avoid" calls attention to the fact that bankruptcy laws change, local jurisdictions may have their own special rules and requirements, and mentions common mistakes people make on their paper-work.

Quality of Legal Forms   **Grade: C‑**

The ***Do-It-Yourself Kit*** includes the official forms you need to file a Chapter 7, 11 or 13 Bankruptcy. The forms are easy to read and reproduce, primarily because they are packaged separately and are not published as a part of the pamphlet. They are not up-to-date, however, and do not reflect all current bankruptcy laws.

Disclaimer

"This product is not intended to provide legal advice. It contains only general information for educational purposes only. Please consult an attorney for your special needs."

Overall   **Grade: D**

You can get a quick feel for bankruptcy proceedings, and

have all the forms you need with ***Do-It-Yourself Kit: Bankruptcy***. You should not rely solely on this product, however, if doing it yourself. $21.95 is a high price for a 28-page pamphlet.

Not Recommended.

Do-It-Yourself Chapter 7 Bankruptcy Kit
SJT Enterprises, Inc., Cleveland, Ohio, 1997
Form Kit, $24.95
(800) 326-7419

Not Recommended

Do-It-Yourself Chapter 7 Bankruptcy Kit provides a bare-bones kit for filing Chapter 7 bankruptcy. The 21-page guide-book contains rudimentary instructions for completing the en-closed bankruptcy forms, and a selection of practice worksheets to fill out before using the actual forms to avoid errors. The kit discusses only Chapter 7 personal bankruptcy. If you have a simple and straightforward Chapter 7 bankruptcy, know the law, and have filled out many of these forms before, you might be able to use this product safely. ***Do-It-Yourself Chapter 7*** contains a state-by-state list of bankruptcy court locations (no addresses or phone numbers are provided), a copy of Section 522 of Title 11, U.S.C., which lists property which is exempt under federal law, a "layman's" description of bankruptcy ex-emptions, and the schedules and legal forms required to file for Chapter 7 proceedings. No state-by-state listing of exemptions is provided.

Accuracy   **Grade: D**
    The information that is included in ***Do-It-Yourself Chap-ter 7*** is fairly accurate, but it does little more than explain the concept of bankruptcy and briefly describe the pro-cess.

Comprehensiveness   **Grade: D**
    Do-It-Yourself Chapter 7 provides minimal informa-tion on the bankruptcy process. The information in this

kit is not sufficient for anyone who is not already well-versed in bankruptcy law to confidently file their own bankruptcy.

Plain Language and Glossary   **Grade: F**
Do-It-Yourself Chapter 7 avoids legalese by not discussing the law and not using any bankruptcy terminology. It does not contain a glossary of definitions of bankruptcy terms.

Easy to Use   **Grade: D**
Do-It-Yourself Chapter 7 is difficult to use for those without legal training. It contains little information on bankruptcy and the instructions are minimal, at best. The kit does include practice copies of the forms for you to use before trying to complete the originals.

Red Flags   **Grade: F**
Do-It-Yourself Chapter 7 does not contain a state-by-state appendix of property exemptions. It only has a copy of Section 522 of Title 11, U.S.C.A., which lists property that is exempt under federal law, and a "layman's" description of the exemption. This is inadequate because every state has variations in the exemptions allowed that can seriously affect your rights. The kit also does not provide information on troublesome areas, potential problems, or what to do in a complex situation.

Quality of Legal Forms   **Grade: C-**
Do-It-Yourself Chapter 7 provides the forms and schedules necessary in filing Chapter 7 bankruptcy, and minimal instructions on how to complete them. We doubt that do-it-yourselfers can complete these forms without help.

Disclaimer

"Publisher cannot guarantee forms in this set are being used for the purpose intended and therefore assumes no responsibility for the proper and correct use. The services of an attorney should be used if there is any variation in the suggested use of this material. This is sold with the understanding that neither the author or the publisher is engaged in rendering legal or financial advice. If either is needed, the services of a qualified attorney or financial expert should be obtained."

Overall   **Grade: D**

Do-It-Yourself Chapter 7 Bankruptcy Kit should not be used by the average consumer to file for Chapter 7 bankruptcy. It does not provide sufficient background information or instruction on the process. $24.95 is a steep price for a 21-page booklet.

Not Recommended.

6

ESTATE PLANNING

According to a recent survey by Roper Starch Worldwide, most Americans who have substantial assets have not taken the necessary steps to plan their estates. Of those who say they have planned their estates, fewer than half have a durable power of attorney (46%), a living will (43%), long-term care insurance (38%), or living trusts (35%). And less than half (48%) have sought financial planning advice about their adult children. Even fewer (41%) have sought advice about aging parents.

The danger of dying without a will (or other estate planning tool, such as a living trust) is that you lose control over who gets your property, who looks after your dependents, and how much of your estate will go to legal fees and taxes. Your wishes about long-term care, treatment for terminal illnesses and even burial arrangements cannot be guaranteed without an estate plan.

An estate plan allows you to control these important decisions, including:
- transfer of property after death;
- care of a dependent spouse or children;
- minimizing or avoiding probate;
- handling your financial or medical decisions if you are incapacitated; and
- reducing taxes and legal fees on your estate.

Planning for one's death may be difficult to think about, but it's never been easier to do. Reliable and affordable products with step-by-step instructions have flooded the marketplace. In this chapter, we review the major and most comprehensive products. Many more titles are listed under the estate planning section of the annotated bibliography (Appendix 2).

One major estate planning tool that most people know about is the will. Living trusts are another estate planning tool that complements the will, and can be used to accomplish many of your goals. The products reviewed in this chapter can also help you create durable powers of attorney and living wills to control medical and financial decisions if you are incapacitated.

Each state has different laws and court decisions that apply to wills, estates, trusts and probate. We have kept this in mind as we evaluated these products.

Wills. The number one reason for writing a will is to leave instructions on how your property should be distributed. But a will can do a lot more—it can name a guardian for minor children, name an executor or personal representative to manage your estate, and authorize your executor to pay taxes owed on your estate.

Most products also allow you to create a testamentary trust in your will. A testamentary trust, also known as a will-trust, allows property to be managed or held for the benefit of family members (for example, a dependent spouse or minor children) and other beneficiaries long after your death.

Living Trusts. A trust is a legal entity that can own, hold and distribute assets (money or property). The major benefit of a living trust is that the property in it isn't considered part of your estate, and therefore bypasses the lengthy and costly probate court proceeding that is triggered by your death. Another benefit is the control and flexibility it can give you over your property.

A living trust is either revocable (meaning it can be changed or revoked at anytime) or irrevocable (the terms of the document cannot be changed after it is signed). A revocable trust allows you total control over what happens to the trust property while you are alive. An irrevocable trust takes control away, but may reward you with large tax savings.

Durable Powers of Attorney and Living Wills. The other major legal decisions that often must be made around the time of your death are triggered by illness or disability. Who will make medical and financial decisions if you can't? There are two basic approaches—designating someone to act for you (a durable power of attorney) or leaving detailed instructions about your wishes (a living will).

A durable power of attorney is a legal document that authorizes another person to make medical and financial decisions on behalf of an incapacitated person. Typically, two separate documents are created (one for health care and one for managing finances), although some states allow one person to make both financial and medical decisions.

A living will is a legal document that instructs your doctors and others about the use, withholding or withdrawal of artificial life-support when incapacitation or terminal illness interferes with your ability to communicate.

Because these legal tools literally deal with life or death issues, you should learn about each approach. There are several products that will help you make sure you are in control, even in your last days.

Of the self-help materials we reviewed, *WillMaker* from Nolo Press stands out as an extraordinary product that truly defines the state-of-the-art for do-it-yourselfers. We believe it is the single best do-it-yourself law product on the market today. Three other products from Nolo Press, *Nolo's Will Book, Living Trust Maker* and *The Financial Power of Attorney Workbook* are exceptional values, and are also HALT Do-it-Yourself Best Buys.

WILLS

WillMaker 6 / WillMaker 7
by Barbara Kate Repa, Stephen Elias, Ralph Warner
Nolo Press, Berkeley, California, 1997
CD-ROM Software for Windows 3.1/95 (tested) and Mac
$69.95
(800) 992-6656

HALT
Do-it-Yourself
Best Buy

WillMaker 6 includes a user's guide, a legal guide, and a cassette tape of an interview with Nolo's Ralph Warner about drafting your own will. The program requires a computer with CD-ROM and can be installed on either Mac or Windows. *WillMaker* allows you to quickly and easily create three kinds of documents: a will, a living will with health care directives, and a document that lays out your wishes about funerals and other final arrangements. The documents you create from *WillMaker* provide the necessary legal instructions for your family, friends and others in case of your death or permanent incapacity. The User's Guide explains the program thoroughly, while the Legal Guide provides detailed information on wills, living wills and funeral arrangements. *WillMaker 7* was released as this book went to production. The changes from *WillMaker 6* are noted below. *WillMaker* is good in all states except Louisiana.

Accuracy   **Grade: A⁺**

WillMaker provides thorough, accurate and complete legal documents that are custom tailored to the special requirements of your state's laws. The program handles most personal and financial situations you are likely to encounter, and customizes your will through an interview process. Minor discrepancies between the program and the printed Legal Guide appeared during testing, but the Read Me file pointed out that the program had been updated to the latest changes in the law while the book had not been. Always check the Read Me files and Nolo's web site for the latest changes affecting *WillMaker*.

Comprehensiveness   **Grade: A**
   WillMaker is an excellent product for accomplishing
most goals you may have when preparing a will. You can
distribute property, name alternate heirs, appoint an executor, name guardians, cancel debts, designate how taxes
are to be paid, and complete most other tasks needed to
deal with death. Just as important, *WillMaker* does not
allow you to do things that are too restrictive, too complex, or which require the assistance of a lawyer.
WillMaker protects you from yourself, and gives you
critical guidance on technically difficult topics such as
making bequests with conditions, writing joint wills, naming co-guardians for children or property, controlling
property after your death and creating complex trusts that
avoid taxes.

   The printed Legal Guide includes a detailed discussion of wills and provides all the information you need to
write one. It includes numerous examples, differences in
state laws, and tells you when you might wish to see a lawyer for more complex matters. The on-screen Legal Guide
is accessible at almost any time during the will writing process whenever you require more information on a topic.
With the hardcopy Legal Guide at your side (or through
the interview process), you definitely won't be in the dark
when you write your will.

   WillMaker 7 also allows you to specify what should
happen to your property if all members of your family die
simultaneously, or if all other family members die before
you. In addition, *WillMaker 7* features a new document,
The Durable Power of Attorney for Finance, which allows
you to name someone to handle your financial affairs if
you become incapacitated.

Plain Language and Glossary   **Grade: A⁺**
   WillMaker avoids almost all legalese and explains will-

writing terminology in the hard copy and on-screen Legal Guides.

Easy to Use   **Grade: A**
WillMaker is extremely easy to use. Installation is through the usual Windows setup routine and once installed, the program takes you through the process of creating your will in a step-by-step fashion. Different people can write wills with the same copy of *WillMaker* by setting up a Profile that keeps track of the documents created by that user.

When you begin, *WillMaker* asks you what kind of document you wish to create (Your Will, Your Healthcare Directives or Your Final Arrangements). Once you've made your selection, *WillMaker* presents an overview of the topic, and explains what you're about to do. It then moves into an interview process that takes you step by step through creating the document. The information you supply is then placed into the completed document at the end of your session.

At almost any time you can click on More Information which accesses the Legal Guide for the topic you're working on. The program also automatically saves a copy of your work so you can't accidentally lose it by forgetting to save.

When you're done, you can display and print your completed document, or export it to your word processor. You should have the printed legal guide with you as a reference when you create a document, although it is not necessary.

Nolo has significantly improved its already excellent interface in *WillMaker 7*, which now displays the extensive legal help on the right side of every interview screen. With this convenient interface, you no longer have to open and close windows to learn about the legal considerations behind each interview question. In addition, users of

Nolo's *Personal RecordKeeper 5* (for Windows only) can link their **WillMaker** file with their *RecordKeeper* database.

Red Flags   **Grade: A**
WillMaker provides detailed information on state differences and carefully points out situations that may require the assistance of an attorney, that may cause confusion, or that may require extra care. Again, the Read Me file contains changes that took place after the software was published.

Quality of Legal Forms   **Grade: A**
WillMaker creates excellent, high-quality documents on your computer's printer.

Disclaimer
"We've done our best to give you useful and accurate information in this software manual. But laws and procedures change frequently and are subject to differing interpretations. If you want legal advice backed by a guarantee, see a lawyer. If you use this software, it's your responsibility to make sure that the facts and general advice contained in it apply to your situation."

Overall   **Grade: A**
WillMaker is an incredibly powerful, comprehensive and easy-to-use software product for making your own will. We believe it is the single best do-it-yourself law product on the market. At $ 69.95, **WillMaker** is an extraordinary value for any consumer.

HALT
Do-it-Yourself
Best Buy

Nolo's Will Book
3rd Edition
by Denis Clifford
Nolo Press, Berkeley, California, 1997
228 pages, $29.95
(800) 992-6656

HALT
Do-it-Yourself
Best Buy

Nolo's Will Book can help you prepare a will—without hiring a lawyer—that is valid in every state except Louisiana. This book allows you to make legally binding decisions about the distribution of your property, who will take care of your minor children and much more. ***Nolo's Will Book*** also provides detailed instructions on proper signing and witnessing of your will to ensure its legality. The product includes tear-out forms and worksheets, and a computer disk with the forms in ASCII text that can be used by any Mac or Windows word processor.

Accuracy   **Grade: A**
   Nolo's Will Book provides accurate and detailed information on will preparation and the law behind it. It provides a wealth of detail about the intricacies of drafting a will, includes a complete overview of information most people will need to write a will, and tells you when to see a lawyer for more complex issues.

Comprehensiveness   **Grade: B⁺**
   Nolo's Will Book is more than sufficient for accomplishing most goals in preparing a will, such as distributing property, naming alternate heirs, appointing an executor, appointing guardians, and disinheriting someone. The book does not cover more complex situations. If the value of your estate triggers federal estate taxes, if you want to establish a complex trust, if you want to arrange long-term care for a beneficiary, or if you fear that someone will con-

test your will, the book suggests that you consult an attorney who specializes in these situations.

Plain Language and Glossary   **Grade: A⁺**

Nolo's Will Book avoids almost all legalese and explains will-writing terminology in the text. An excellent glossary of definitions is included for easy reference.

Easy to Use   **Grade: A**

Nolo's Will Book is very well-organized and straightforward. The book's chapters are designed to be read sequentially, and provide thorough, easy-to-understand background information on property laws. After reading the material, you complete worksheets with information about beneficiaries, real estate, and personal property for later entry on the will forms. *Nolo's Will Book* also provides optional clauses that cover other situations. The computer disk contains the forms in ASCII text and can be used on any computer with a word processor. *Nolo's Will Book* also provides guidance on the formalities of signing and witnessing your will to make sure it's valid in your state.

Red Flags   **Grade: A**

Prominent warnings are placed throughout *Nolo's Will Book* whenever there is an issue that may cause problems, is too complex for this book, or requires the help of a qualified professional.

Quality of Legal Forms   **Grade: A**

Nolo's Will Book provides the will forms, "create-your-own-will clauses," and worksheets you'll need to draft your will. The forms are very legible, perforated for easy removal, and will produce excellent photocopies. You can use a computer to prepare the final version of your will, or use a typewriter.

Disclaimer

"We've done our best to give you useful and accurate information in this book. But laws and procedures change frequently and are subject to differing interpretations. If you want legal advice backed by a guarantee, see a lawyer. If you use this book, it's your personal responsibility to make sure that the facts and general advice contained in it are applicable to your situation."

Overall   **Grade: A**

If you want to write your own will and do not have any of the complex issues that require professional help, *Nolo's Will Book* is an excellent resource. At $29.95, it is an exceptional value for do-it-yourselfers.

HALT
Do-it-Yourself
Best Buy

Prepare Your Own Will: The National Will Kit
4th Edition
by Daniel Sitarz
Nova Publishing, Carbondale, Illinois, 1996
246 pages, $27.95
(800) 748-1175   ***Recommended***

Prepare Your Own Will: The National Will Kit provides
information on how to write a legally valid will in all 50 states
and the District of Columbia. The book covers estate planning
topics, information on what you need to do before you get
started, and step-by-step instructions for writing your own will.
Information on changing your will, writing a living will and a
durable power of attorney is also included. The book ends with
a state-specific appendix, glossary and index. A Windows form
disk is attached to the back cover, and a Mac disk is available
upon request.

Accuracy   **Grade: A⁻**
   Prepare Your Own Will provides an accurate and comprehensive discussion of will preparation. The book
   clearly outlines your options, steers you through the drafting process, and alerts you to what can and cannot be
   included in your will. The appendix at the back of the
   book, which addresses state laws relating to wills, is a nice
   touch and will help you draft a will that is valid in your
   state.

Comprehensiveness   **Grade: B**
   When it comes down to it, drafting your will is the easy
   part. It's the work you need to do beforehand that's time-
   consuming, although not necessarily difficult. ***Prepare***
   Your Own Will makes the job a bit easier by explaining
   what needs to be done, and then having you complete two

questionnaires. The first covers your property—what you have and how it's owned. The second covers your beneficiaries—who gets what and when. Immediately following that is a chapter entitled Information for Executor. Once these steps are completed, the rest is a matter of choosing the right clauses and adding the correct information.

Prepare Your Own Will allows you to create a customized will by choosing from a series of mandatory and optional clauses, or skipping to pre-assembled wills that have made certain assumptions (like you're married).

Limited information (one page) is devoted to a discussion of taxes (federal estate, state inheritance and gift) and their impact on estate planning. The discussion does not include the latest information available, because it was published a year before the new tax act. An insert, updating the reader on recent tax law changes, could have solved that problem.

Plain Language and Glossary   **Grade: B**

Prepare Your Own Will uses plain language in the text, although avoidable legalese creeps in here and there. A small glossary of legal terms covers the basics, but leaves out many of the legal terms commonly used in estate planning and taxes—for example, *gross estate*, *issue*, and *principal* are not defined.

Easy to Use   **Grade: B**

Prepare Your Own Will is easy to understand and use. Step-by-step instructions are included for completing a customized will or a pre-assembled will. The addition of a form disk to this publication makes it easier to generate wills, although it is a bit cumbersome to have to open a new file for each clause and then copy that clause into a different file that contains your will. Those without computers have to type their will.

Red Flags   **Grade: A**
   Prepare Your Own Will includes warnings about when
   legal help should be sought and when state laws may vary.
   It also uses boldface lettering to call your attention to the
   specific clauses each will must include to be valid.

Quality of Legal Forms   **Grade: B⁺**

   Prepare Your Own Will includes forms that can easily
   be photocopied, retyped or computer-generated by do-it-
   yourselfers.

Disclaimer
   "Because of possible unanticipated changes in governing
   statutes and case law relating to the application of any information contained in this book, the author, publisher,
   and any and all persons or entities involved in any way in
   the preparation, publication, sale or distribution of this
   book disclaim all responsibility for the legal effects or consequences of any document prepared or action taken in
   reliance upon information contained in this book. No representations, either express or implied, are made or given
   regarding the legal consequences of the use of any information contained in this book. Purchasers and persons
   intending to use this book for the preparation of any legal
   documents are advised to check specifically on the current applicable laws in any jurisdiction in which they intend
   the documents to be effective."

Overall   **Grade: B⁺**
   Prepare Your Own Will is a solid publication to use
   for those wanting a simple will. At $27.95, it is an excel-
   lent value for consumers who have simple, straightforward
   estate planning needs. For those with more complicated
   needs, or those with complex tax considerations, a more
   in-depth publication should be consulted.

                                    Recommended.

Good Value

How to Make Your Own Will
by Mark Warda
Sourcebooks, Inc., Naperville, Illinois, 1998
144 pages, $12.95
(800) 226-5291

How to Make Your Own Will is designed to help you write a will that is valid in every state without the expense or delay of hiring a lawyer. The book is designed to allow those with simple estates to quickly distribute their property according to their wishes. *Make Your Own Will* contains basic will forms with examples, and discusses many common legal concepts, such as the different ways you hold property, "pay on death" accounts, appointing a guardian for a minor, living wills, and organ donation. It also contains state-specific information to help make sure your will conforms to the laws that apply where you live.

Accuracy   **Grade: B**
> *Make Your Own Will* provides accurate, but occasionally overly general, information on will preparation and the law behind it. It has a good overview of the information you need to write your will, and tells you when you should seek professional help for more complex matters.

Comprehensiveness   **Grade: C⁺**
> Although sufficient for writing a simple will, *Make Your Own Will* is sometimes too general in the way it presents the information. The book will help you understand how inheritance laws, property rules, beneficiaries, bequests and how marriage, divorce, and children affect your will. *Make Your Own Will* should not be used in situations that go beyond the use of a simple will, such as if the will

could be contested, complicated estates or estates that
trigger the federal estate tax.

Plain Language and Glossary   **Grade: C**
Make Your Own Will avoids almost all legalese and
provides accurate, but sometimes over-simplified definitions of will-writing terminology in the text. *Make Your
Own Will* does not contain a glossary of definitions of
will-writing terminology.

Easy to Use   **Grade: B**
Make Your Own Will is well-organized and straightforward. The book's chapters are designed to be read
sequentially, and provide background information on inheritance and property laws. You're asked to read the
material before filling out the forms to make sure you understand important legal concepts. *Make Your Own Will*
includes 16 different forms that cover most simple situations. Also included are forms for codicils (amendments
to your will), self-proving affidavits, and sample forms that
are already completed. Special attention is provided to
signing and witnessing your will to make sure it's valid in
your state. The book also contain an appendix that lists
state laws that may affect your will, along with citations.

Red Flags   **Grade: B⁻**
Make Your Own Will identifies situations that may
cause problems, and generally recommends that you consult an attorney whenever an issue is complex. State
differences are pointed out and listed in the appendix.

Quality of Legal Forms   **Grade: B⁻**
How to Make Your Own Will provides 16 will forms
(two copies of each), assorted codicils, and self-proving
affidavits. The forms are very legible, but are not perforated for easy removal. They will produce excellent
photocopies.

Disclaimer

"This publication is designed to provide accurate and authoritative information in regard to the subject matter covered. It is sold with the understanding that the publisher is not engaged in rendering legal, accounting, or other professional service. If legal advice or other expert assistance is required, the services of a competent professional person should be sought."

Overall   **Grade: C⁺**

How to Make Your Own Will is a good resource for those who would like to write a simple will. At $12.95, it is a real bargain for those on a tight budget, who lack computers, or who don't need more than a boilerplate will.

Good Value.

Do-It-Yourself Kit:
Last Will & Testament

E-Z Legal Forms, Inc., Deerfield Beach, Florida,
1994/1992 (forms), Form Kit, $21.95
(954) 480-8933

Not Recommended

Do-It-Yourself Kit: Last Will & Testament includes a small information pamphlet and the forms needed to create a very basic will. A series of other one-page forms—Notification List, Funeral Request, Document Locator, and Insurance Record—let you record supplemental information for the executor of your will. The kit also includes a short glossary.

Accuracy   **Grade: C⁻**

Last Will & Testament gives an extremely basic overview of what you should know about writing a will. While the information is accurate, the lack of detail may lead some unsuspecting consumers into drafting a will without an adequate understanding of the law.

Comprehensiveness   **Grade: D**

Last Will & Testament is far from comprehensive. The topic of writing a will is covered in less than 12 pages and is incomplete. For example, the *Kit* tells you what the legal requirements are for writing a valid will ("be of legal age and sound mind"), but does not explain what that means. Other important information is handled in a similarly superficial fashion.

Many do-it-yourself consumers will be offended by the *Last Will & Testament's* presumptions that lawyers must be involved. For example, when discussing whom to appoint as a personal representative, this product states "Typically, a spouse, relative or close friend serves as personal representative, as the duties are not difficult and your personal representative will retain an attorney to process the necessary probate forms."

Plain Language and Glossary   **Grade: D**

Although the information pamphlet is written primarily in plain language, many legal terms and concepts are used but not defined in the text or in the glossary.

Easy to Use   **Grade: C‑**

The *Last Will & Testament* provides clean and legible pre-printed forms that can be photocopied and completed fairly easily, but lacks detailed step-by-step guidance that do-it-yourselfers need. For example, instead of "type your name" as the kit instructs, it could state "type your full legal name." To its credit, the *Kit* explains the different parts of a will with simple language and a sample will is included. We were also surprised to find, with a 1994 copyright date, information on federal tax law changes that went into effect in 1998. Those who need more detail in their will, however, will have to look elsewhere since only one type of will is provided.

Red Flags   **Grade: D**

The *Last Will & Testament* suggests that a lawyer be consulted if the kit doesn't address your needs or you're not comfortable preparing your own documents. It does not offer warnings about potential pitfalls in drafting or executing the document.

Quality of Legal Forms   **Grade: C**

The basic will form is easy to read and reproduce, primarily because it is packaged separately and not published as a part of the pamphlet.

Disclaimer

"It is understood that by using this kit, you are acting as your own attorney. Neither the author, publisher, distributor nor retailer are engaged in rendering legal, accounting or other professional services. Accordingly, the publisher, author, distributor, and retailer shall have neither liability nor responsibility to any party for any loss or damage caused or alleged to be caused by the use of this product.

Overall   **Grade: D**

Do-it-yourself consumers should probably take a pass on ***Do-It-Yourself Kit: Last Will & Testament*** given what's on the market for the same price. $21.95 is a very steep price for a 17-page product. A computer version of this product—***Last Will & Testament Software***—is also available on CD-ROM or computer disk for Windows 3.1/95. Although it is easy to install, the program's interface is extremely basic, asking you for an item of information and then adding it to a boilerplate form. The form may then be edited and printed. No legal background help or information is provided, nor is a legal dictionary. The program is also slow (on a Pentium, though the requirements list a 386 or better) and feels clunky and rough.

Not Recommended.

TRUSTS

Living Trust Maker 2.0
Nolo Press, Berkeley, California, 1998
Software, $79.95
(800) 992-6656

HALT
Do-it-Yourself
Best Buy

Living Trust Maker 2.0 includes a 200+ page "legal manual," and a CD-ROM that provides a tutorial on how to use the software. It includes demos for three of Nolo's other products, *WillMaker, Small Business Pro* and *Recordkeeper. Living Trust Maker* also contains information about registering as a user so you can keep informed of changes in the law or to the program. *Living Trust Maker* is good in all states except Louisiana.

Accuracy   **Grade: A**
   Living Trust Maker provides thorough, accurate and complete information on creating revocable living trusts for individuals and married couples. People who register with Nolo will be contacted about recent changes in the law that affect this program.

Comprehensiveness   **Grade: A**
   Living Trust Maker is packed with information on the most popular probate avoidance tool, the revocable living trust. The legal manual covers virtually everything you need to know, not only about trusts, but the other methods for passing property after death, including the advantages and disadvantages of each. Other estate planning documents are covered as well, including information on durable powers of attorney and living wills.

Plain Language and Glossary   **Grade: A⁻**
   Living Trust Maker uses legalese only when absolutely necessary and fully explains it in the text. The lack of a

glossary listing and defining legal terminology in one easy-to-access location is the one shortcoming we identified in this product.

Easy to Use   **Grade: A**

Living Trust Maker is easy to install and extremely easy to use. As Nolo claims, you can create a legally valid, state-specific trust in 10 minutes; although you're encouraged to spend an evening or two acquainting yourself with the material in the hefty legal manual and pulling together the necessary personal information. If you need technical assistance with operating the software, Nolo provides it free of charge.

You create your trust through an interview. Along the way, windows pop up that ask you to make decisions by selecting a particular answer or by filling in information in a dialog box. More detailed information about the section of the trust you're working on (for example, selecting beneficiaries) is available by clicking on a Legal Help button, or on specific listings of topics that pop up from time to time. The trust is completed behind the scene (or screen) as you answer seven sets of questions. You can review previous pages at any time by hitting a Back button, but you must go sequentially forward before getting to the last step. Before printing the trust documents, you can review them and go back to make changes.

Red Flags   **Grade: A**

Areas that warrant special attention are flagged in the Legal Manual with special icons. Readers are told when they may need to contact a lawyer, potential pitfalls in drafting and when other resources should be consulted.

Quality of Legal Forms   **Grade: A**

Living Trust Maker allows you to produce great looking, state-specific, customized living trust documents.

Disclaimer

"We've done our best to give you useful and accurate information in this book. But laws and procedures change frequently and are subject to differing interpretations. If you want legal advice backed by a guarantee, see a lawyer. If you use this book, it's your responsibility to make sure that the facts and general advice contained in it are applicable to your situation."

Overall   **Grade: A**

If you know that you want to set up a living trust, *Living Trust Maker* is an accurate, complete and easy-to-use way to get through the process. At $79.95, it is an exceptional value for anyone who wants to write their own living trust, which can easily cost over $1,000 when drafted by attorneys.

HALT
Do-it-Yourself
Best Buy

Avoid Probate:
Make Your Own Living Trust
3rd Edition
by Denis Clifford
Nolo Press, Berkeley, California, 1998
336 pages, $24.95
(800) 992-6656

Recommended

Avoid Probate: Make Your Own Living Trust provides a complete overview of revocable living trusts, with step-by-step instructions for preparing and transferring property into a trust to limit or completely avoid taxes on your estate. The book also includes chapters on estate planning, wills, "if you need expert help," a glossary of estate planning terms, and an appendix of 12 different fill-in-the-blank forms.

Accuracy   **Grade: A**
   Avoid Probate provides comprehensive and accurate information on drafting and "funding" (placing your property into) a living trust in every state except Louisiana. Up-to-date information is also given on the general topic of estate planning, and how a living trust can fit into your plan.

Comprehensiveness   **Grade: A⁻**
   Avoid Probate is a hefty book with 17 chapters and 12 fill-in-the-blank forms that allow you to complete three different kinds of trusts: a basic trust for one person; a basic trust for two persons; and a trust for married couples.
   The first four chapters provide a broad, but excellent overview, explaining living trusts, the different kinds available and answering common questions, for example, "Will a living trust shield my property from creditors?" Throughout ***Avoid Probate***, the reader will find useful real-life examples, as well as charts, graphics, and screened boxed

information that make the book not only easy on the eyes but a pleasure to read.

For couples, *Avoid Probate* includes information and a form for the tax-saving "AB Trust." The meat of the book, however, is devoted to discussing the mechanics of executing a trust, and helping you think about what property you want to put in a trust, who will manage the trust and who should benefit from its assets.

· In addition to chapters on how to prepare, place property into and register the trust, *Avoid Probate* includes great after-the-fact chapters not usually found in self-help publications. For example, *Living With Your Living Trust* discusses when and if you need to make changes to your trust, and *After a Grantor Dies* provides specific advice on a trustee's responsibilities. *Avoid Probate* also includes good estate planning information, particularly on wills, and a chapter that helps you decide if expert help is needed.

Plain Language and Glossary   **Grade: A**

The text and fill-in-the-blank documents are written in plain language. Legal terms are used only when unavoidable and explained in the text. An extensive and excellent glossary clearly explains trust terminology.

Easy to Use   **Grade: B⁻**

While we found *Avoid Probate* very easy to read and understand, the step-by-step directions are a bit cumbersome. Although you are asked to follow a 12-step plan, not all steps are used in all of the trusts, which is sometimes confusing. The forms at the back of the book have circled numbers next to some clauses which correspond to the 12-step instruction plan, which requires you to constantly flip back and forth between the document and Chapter 10.

Red Flags   **Grade: A**
Areas that warrant special attention are flagged with
special icons, and *Avoid Probate* tells you when you
need to consult a professional or consult other resources.

Quality of Legal Forms   **Grade: B**
The forms included in *Avoid Probate* are really
worksheets that you complete, then have typed and proofread. The quality of the finished product, therefore,
depends a lot on the accuracy of the typist.

Disclaimer
"We've done our best to give you useful and accurate information in this book. But laws and procedures change
frequently and are subject to differing interpretations. If
you want legal advice backed by a guarantee, see a lawyer. If you use this book, it's your responsibility to make
sure that the facts and general advice contained in it are
applicable to your situation."

Overall   **Grade: B⁺**
Avoid Probate: Make Your Own Living Trust offers a wealth of good and up-to-date information about
living trusts in easy to understand language. The publication would be enhanced, and easier to use, if it came
with a form disk. At $24.95, it is an excellent value for
consumers who are not computer literate, and who can
type or hire a typist.

Recommended.

LivingTrustBuilder
4th Edition
by Craig G. Christensen and John E. Barrus
JIAN, Inc., Mountain View, California, 1995
390 pages with Software, $49.00
(800) 346-5426

Recommended

LivingTrustBuilder is a complete reference guide that allows you to write your own living trust quickly and easily. The book provides thorough background information on what living trusts are, how they work, how to create one and how they compare to other estate planning options. The software contains 32 living trusts, related forms and worksheets in a template format for use with almost any word processor for Windows or Mac.

Accuracy   **Grade: B**

LivingTrustBuilder provides accurate, but sometimes overly general, information on the creation and use of living trusts. Although the book provides more than adequate information, you are constantly told that all work must be checked by an attorney.

Comprehensiveness   **Grade: B**

LivingTrustBuilder provides the information you need to know to create your own living trust. It fully discusses the different ways to avoid probate and why a living trust may be best for you. The living trust information is quite thorough and provides excellent background information on how to create a living trust with the provided forms. In addition, the book discusses how to plan for the transfer of your business after your death. The 32 forms cover most common situations. The book always recommends that you see an attorney to check any work you have done.

Plain Language and Glossary   **Grade: A**
LivingTrustBuilder does an excellent job of using plain
language rather than legalese. It also contains a terrific
glossary of definitions of trust-related terminology.

Easy to Use   **Grade: A**
LivingTrustBuilder is well-organized and easy to use.
After reading the background information, you choose
which forms are required for your situation. The forms
are contained as templates for your word processor and
are easily edited for your use. Detailed instructions and
explanations are included within the forms for every blank
you must fill out. These instructions are then deleted before you print your final version. The forms are also
included in their entirety in the text of the reference
manual, so book and software can easily be used together.

Red Flags   **Grade: C**
LivingTrustBuilder does not highlight possible problem areas with bold face warnings or in some other
prominent way, but it does include information about possible problems. However, this product recommends that
you have your work examined by an attorney for everything. This approach may help the publisher avoid
unauthorized practice of law charges, but it is tedious to
consumers who purchased the product to do it themselves.

Quality of Legal Forms   **Grade: A**
The forms produced through your word processor by using the supplied templates are very attractive and easy to
read. Since you use your own word processor, it is easy
to change the font or font size and customize the style of
your documents.

Disclaimer
"The purpose of this software product is to assist you in
the preparation of sample estate planning documents. You
must have these documents reviewed and approved by an

estate planning attorney to ensure that the documents meet your particular needs, as well as to ensure that the documents conform to state and federal law.

Do not use these documents without consulting an estate planning attorney.

JIAN and the authors of the software do not represent or guarantee that these documents are appropriate for your needs, satisfy any provision of state or federal law, or will have any particular state or federal tax effect. By using *LivingTrustBuilder*, you acknowledge that you will have the documents reviewed by a qualified attorney."

Overall   **Grade: B**

LivingTrustBuilder is a good resource to use in creating a living trust, but if you follow the publisher's recommendation, you must have everything examined by an attorney, which may negate a significant portion of the cost savings in doing the work yourself. At $49.00, *LivingTrustBuilder* is, nonetheless, an excellent value for do-it-yourself consumers.

Recommended.

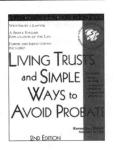

Living Trusts and Simple Ways to Avoid Probate

2nd Edition
by Karen Ann Rolcik
Sourcebooks, Inc., Naperville, Illinois, 1998
159 pages, $19.95
(800) 226-5291

Good Value

Living Trusts and Simple Ways to Avoid Probate is designed to help you create a living trust, and provides information on other options you have for avoiding probate. The book explains probate, the different ways of holding property, gifts, and living trusts. *Simple Ways to Avoid Probate* also contains forms and worksheets for creating a living trust and the appropriate tax forms.

Accuracy   **Grade: B**

Simple Ways to Avoid Probate provides accurate, although general, information on alternatives to probate. It deals with living trusts in much more detail, providing background information, and clearly identifying situations when you should seek professional help.

Comprehensiveness   **Grade: B**

Simple Ways to Avoid Probate provides a good introduction to the alternatives available to help avoid probate with a special emphasis on living trusts. The discussion is quite thorough and provides excellent background on how to create a living trust with the provided forms. The forms in the book are not for people with estates valued at an amount that will trigger federal estate taxes, or those who have unusual assets such as royalty interests, partnership interests or interests in trusts or annuities. Nor should they be used if there are complicated beneficiary distributions or conditions you wish to include in your living trust.

Plain Language and Glossary   **Grade: C⁺**

Simple Ways to Avoid Probate avoids almost all legalese and usually explains legal trust terminology in the text. The lack of a glossary that explains trust terminology is a major shortcoming in this product.

Easy to Use   **Grade: C⁺**

Simple Ways to Avoid Probate is well organized and concise. After discussing different ways to avoid probate, the book covers living trusts in some detail, explaining everything you need to fill out the forms and providing examples. The forms are easy to understand with terminology explained in the text. The lack of step-by-step instructions makes this product a bit difficult to use, but many of the forms simply require names and dates.

Red Flags   **Grade: C⁺**

Simple Ways to Avoid Probate clearly identifies issues that are too complex for this book, and recommends the use of an attorney. State-by-state differences are also discussed in the text with statutory references when necessary.

Quality of Legal Forms   **Grade: B**

Simple Ways to Avoid Probate provides 13 living trusts and related forms and six tax forms with explanations. The forms are very legible, but are not perforated for easy removal. They will produce excellent photocopies.

Disclaimer

"This publication is designed to provide accurate and authoritative information in regard to the subject matter covered. It is sold with the understanding that the publisher is not engaged in rendering legal, accounting, or other professional service. If legal advice or other expert assistance is required, the services of a competent professional person should be sought."

Overall   **Grade: C⁺**
Living Trusts and Simple Ways to Avoid Probate
is a good resource for information on alternatives to probate and living trusts. At $19.95, it provides the basic information and forms for do-it-yourselfers who want to create a simple living trust.

Good Value.

Do-It-Yourself Kit: Living Trust

E-Z Legal Forms, Deerfield Beach, Florida, 1998
Form Kit, $18.95
(954) 480-8933

Not Recommended

The ***Do-It-Yourself Kit: Living Trust*** claims it will allow you to create your own living trust and save hundreds of dollars on legal fees. The kit contains a 17-page instruction booklet and forms, and is advertised as valid in all 50 states.

Accuracy   **Grade: C**

Living Trust provides an accurate, but extremely limited overview of living trusts.

Comprehensiveness   **Grade: D**

The instruction book in ***Living Trust*** provides only a bare minimum of information on the preparation and use of living trusts. The instructions briefly discuss the advantages and disadvantages of living trusts, how a trust relates to your will, how to set up and manage a living trust, tax issues, and how to revoke a living trust. Although many topics are covered, the information provided is very general and cursory. The instructions do point out states that may have problems with trust preparation, and recommend the use of an attorney.

Plain Language and Glossary   **Grade: C⁻**

Living Trust avoids legalese and explains some legal terminology in the text, but the forms included in the kit are chock full of legal jargon. It includes a very brief and general glossary.

Easy to Use   **Grade: F**
Living Trust is confusing to use, due to the brevity of the
kit. There are no instructions for the forms themselves
and you have to muddle through, filling in the blanks and
trying to decipher the legalese. No examples are given.

Red Flags   **Grade: D**
Living Trust points out the most obvious problems you
may encounter in different states based on their property
and probate laws, and recommends that you hire a lawyer to deal with anything else.

Quality of Legal Forms   **Grade: B**
Living Trust provides nine basic living trust and related
forms. The forms are clearly printed and loose-leaf, so
no tearing or cutting is necessary for their use, and they
will produce excellent photocopies.

Disclaimer
"It is understood that by using this kit, you are acting as
your own attorney. Neither the author, publisher, distributor nor retailer are engaged in rendering legal, accounting
or other professional services. Accordingly, the publisher,
author, distributor and retailer shall have neither liability
nor responsibility to any party for any loss or damage
caused or alleged to be caused by the use of this product."

Overall   **Grade: D**
The **Do-It-Yourself Kit: Living Trust** provides the bar-
est minimum of information required to prepare a living
trust and should not be used by do-it-yourselfers. $18.95
is a high price for a 17-page instruction book. A computer
version of this product—**Living Trust Software**—is also
available on CD-ROM or computer disk for Windows 3.1/
95. Although easy to install, the program's interface is extremely basic, asking you for an item of information and
then adding it to your form. The form may then be edited
and printed. No legal background or information is pro-

vided, nor is a legal dictionary. The program is also slow (on a Pentium, though the requirements list a 386 or better), and feels clunky and rough.

Not Recommended.

The Living Trust:
A Cure for the Agony of Probate
by Vijay Fadia
Homestead Publishing Co., Torrance, California, 1996
193 pages, $39.95
(213) 214-3559   **Not Recommended**

The Living Trust: A Cure for the Agony of Probate is a
193-page book that provides an overview, step-by-step instructions and fill-in-the-blank forms for creating, funding, revoking
and amending revocable living trusts. The book also includes
a fill-in-the-blank "pour-over will," various estate planning
worksheets, and a glossary of terms. A PC disk now comes with
the publication, but was not included with the review copy.

Accuracy   **Grade: D**
   We found the legal discussions in *The Living Trust* to
   be overly broad and sometimes misleading, because
   details are left out. The trust forms include standard
   boilerplate language.

Comprehensiveness   **Grade: D**
   The Living Trust does not comprehensively discuss the
   probate process, the revocable living trust or other probate avoidance tools. So much effort is devoted to trashing
   probate that critical details are omitted—such as the fact
   that most states have now adopted "unsupervised adminis-
   tration" and that it is possible to probate an estate without
   the help of an attorney. The author fails to even mention
   that there are more probate avoidance tools than just the
   two discussed in his book. The discussion of trusts is not
   thorough (less than eight pages) and leaves out many details routinely included in other products (such as the kind
   of property you should or should not put into a living trust,

selecting beneficiaries and leaving property to minors).

The trust forms allow you to create a very simple living trust for an individual or married couple. The married couple's trust is not a tax-savings marital or "A-B" trust. It is basically the same trust an individual uses except it names both spouses in the trust. When one spouse dies, the surviving spouse continues to manage and benefit from the trust's assets until death. If the assets exceed the maximum amount allowed by the marital deduction, the estate will owe taxes.

Plain Language and Glossary   **Grade: D**
Although the text of the book uses plain language, formal and legalistic language is used in the trust forms. A glossary of terms is included, but it does not cover many of the legal terms used in the forms. Much of the legalese is neither explained in the text nor covered in the glossary.

Easy to Use   **Grade: D**
Rudimentary step-by-step instructions are included—the reader is instructed to fill in the blanks, and to have the form notarized and copied.

Red Flags   **Grade: F**
While readers are told when they may need to contact a lawyer, potential pitfalls in drafting a living trust are not identified.

Quality of Legal Forms   **Grade: D**
The preprinted, tear-out, fill-in-the-blank forms provided by this book do not have a very professional appearance.

Disclaimer
"Although care has been taken to ensure the accuracy and utility of the information and forms contained in this book, neither the publisher nor the author assumes any liability in connection with any use thereof. This publication is sold with the understanding that the publisher is not

engaged in rendering legal, accounting, or other professional service. This book should not be used as a substitute for professional assistance essential to planning your estate. Consult a competent professional for applicability to your situation or to answer your specific questions."

Overall   **Grade: D**
The Living Trust: A Cure for the Agony of Probate lacks detail and provides overly simplistic trust forms that do not fit most consumers' needs. At $39.95, it is not a good value.

                                        Not Recommended.

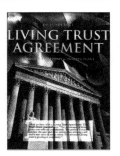

Do-It-Yourself: Living Trust Agreement Kit
SJT Enterprises, Inc., Cleveland, Ohio, 1996
Form Kit, $14.95
(800) 326-7419

Not Recommended

Do-It-Yourself: Living Trust Agreement includes a small information pamphlet and the forms needed to create a very basic living trust for a single or married individual. A series of other one-page forms are included: Exhibit A, Exhibit B, Notary Public form and Revocation of Revocable Living Trust. The kit comes with a PC form disk.

Accuracy   Grade: F
Living Trust Agreement gives an extremely basic over-view of a living trust, which, while broad and technically accurate, fails to discuss many important details. These omissions make it a potentially mislead-ing and dangerous product. For example, under the one-paragraph discussion Trusts and Taxes, the author states "Although trusts can avoid probate, they do not avoid estate or gift taxes as a general rule. Other tech-niques are recommended for avoiding estate and gift taxes." What the author fails to tell you is that living trusts *can* be set up to reduce or completely eliminate estate taxes, just not the trusts this kit provides.

Comprehensiveness   Grade: F
Living Trust Agreement devotes only eight pages to describing the living trust and how to create one. The discussion of other topics is even more superficial, and completely omits critical information you need to make correct choices about your estate. For example, the kit is silent on when you might not need a trust, what drawbacks

there are to having a trust, what kind of property can be put into a trust, what the federal estate tax levels are, and how those taxes can be avoided with living trusts. The kit fails to describe the duties of a trustee, whom you might want to select as a beneficiary, and how old your beneficiaries should be before they can collect assets.

Plain Language and Glossary   **Grade: D**

Although written primarily in plain language, the kit uses many legal terms and concepts, but does not define them in the text. Nor does it include a glossary.

Easy to Use   **Grade: D**

Living Trust Agreement appears easy to use, because it's written in such a simplistic fashion. The step-by-step instructions are inadequate—a list of five steps for filling out the forms with one-sentence directions.

Red Flags   **Grade: F**

Living Trust Agreement suggests that a lawyer be consulted if the kit doesn't address your needs or you're not comfortable preparing your own documents. It does not offer warnings about potential pitfalls in drafting or executing the document.

Quality of Legal Forms   **Grade: D**

Users have to cut the legal forms out of the pamphlet or photocopy them because perforated pages are not provided. The lack of directions for completing the forms means that most people will have a tough time producing sound trust documents with this product.

Disclaimer

"This material is sold with the understanding that neither the author or the publisher is engaged in rendering legal advice. If legal advice is needed, the services of an attorney should be obtained. BY FILLING OUT THE FORMS IN THIS BOOK, YOU ARE ACTING AS YOUR OWN

ATTORNEY. The author and/or publisher of this book and forms are not liable for material in this publication. The only guarantee this publication holds is to the purchase price."

Overall   **Grade: F**

We believe that ***Do-It-Yourself: Living Trust Agreement*** is a misleading and potentially dangerous product. At $14.95, its 8-page booklet provides little of value to most consumers and may result in real problems upon your death.

Not Recommended.

POWERS OF ATTORNEY
AND LIVING WILLS

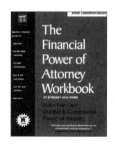

The Financial Power of Attorney Workbook

1st Edition
by Shae Irving
Nolo Press, Berkeley, California, 1997
250 pages, $24.95
(800) 992-6656

HALT
Do-it-Yourself
Best Buy

The Financial Power of Attorney Workbook provides detailed background information, step-by-step instructions and forms for preparing durable and conventional powers of attorney. These documents allow you to name someone to take care of your financial affairs (a conventional power of attorney ends if you become incapacitated, while a durable power of attorney remains in effect). Power of attorney forms are included in the book and on a computer disk that can be used by any PC running Windows or DOS. Mac users need PC Exchange software (which is now built into the operating system).

Accuracy   **Grade: A**

The Workbook offers accurate and up-to-date information on creating both durable and conventional powers of attorney. Although the basic financial power of attorney form offered in the book is valid in all 50 states, state-specific financial powers of attorney forms are included for Alaska, Arizona, the District of Columbia, New Mexico, North Carolina and Oklahoma. Statutes governing powers of attorney are also listed for every state.

Comprehensiveness   **Grade: A**

The Workbook provides an excellent explanation of powers of attorney, and includes the forms you need to create one. This book also includes forms that grant a broad range of powers, and others that grant only limited powers. You

can create a durable power of attorney for finances, a conventional power of attorney for finances, a power of
attorney for real estate, and a power of attorney for child
care.

Lots of information and examples help you understand
when each kind of power of attorney should and should
not be used. If you need additional help or want to do fur-
ther research on the subject, there's a chapter entitled Help
Beyond the Book, that guides you in completing your own
legal research.

The book also provides forms for revoking a power of
attorney and allowing the resignation of the person you've
appointed to be your attorney-in-fact. Instructions are
also provided that can be photocopied and given to your
attorney-in-fact. *The Workbook* is packed with useful tips,
such as suggesting that you check with the bank or other
financial institution to see if it provides its own power of
attorney form before creating a limited durable power of
attorney for finances.

Plain Language and Glossary   **Grade: B⁺**

The text and fill-in-the-blank documents are written in plain
language. Legalese is used only when necessary and is
usually explained. The book does not include a separate
glossary of legal terms, but does define "important terms"
in Chapter 1, although some of the legal terms used in the
actual documents—such as proxy, indemnify and gross
negligence—are not fully explained.

Easy to Use   **Grade: A**

This book is easy to understand and use. Detailed and easy
to follow step-by-step directions are given for completing,
signing and notarizing the forms or for producing computer generated forms.

Red Flags   **Grade: A**

Special icons highlight areas that warrant attention, telling
readers about potential pitfalls, when they need to contact

a lawyer, when other resources should be consulted, and whether they can skip or skim a section.

Quality of Legal Forms   **Grade: A**
Readers can complete their selected form and have it typed and proofread, or they can produce a word-processed version from the computer disk, editing out extraneous material.

Disclaimer
"We've done our best to give you useful and accurate information in this book. But laws and procedures change frequently and are subject to differing interpretations. If you want legal advice backed by a guarantee, see a lawyer. If you use this book, it's your responsibility to make sure that the facts and general advice contained in it are applicable to your situation."

Overall   **Grade: A**
The Financial Power of Attorney Workbook does an excellent job of explaining powers of attorney and provides you with the tools you need to create your own. At $24.95, it is a valuable reference and do-it-yourself guide for any self-help library.

HALT
Do-it-Yourself
Best Buy

How to Write Your Own Living Will

by Edward A. Haman
Sourcebooks, Naperville, Illinois, 1997
148 pages, $9.95
(800) 226-5291

Recommended

How to Write Your Own Living Will provides an overview of living wills, as well as step-by-step instructions and forms for preparing a living will in all 50 states and the District of Columbia. This book includes an index and a state-by-state listing of laws that apply to living wills.

Accuracy   **Grade: A**
> *Your Own Living Will* provides accurate and up-to-date information on creating living wills, including each state's laws on living wills and state-specific forms for 38 states. A basic form for residents of the remaining states is also provided. Although readers who do not have access to a state-specific form can use the basic form, they're encouraged to check their state's statutes or code because "legislators could adopt a form at any time."

Comprehensiveness   **Grade: A⁻**
> *Your Own Living Will* provides a thorough explanation of living wills, and how they differ from a durable power of attorney for health care. The book discusses how these tools have changed over the years to deal with more complicated issues—such as women who are terminally ill and pregnant, and individuals in vegetative states, and how living wills can now be used to enforce your decision on life-prolonging procedures.
>
> > *Your Own Living Will* includes state-specific information and a state-specific form is included for each state

that has a living will law. It also provides citations to the state statutes, along with information about whether a doctor's certification is required, the kinds of conditions covered by the form, and whether the document has to be witnessed.

Your Own Living Will devotes an entire chapter to lawyers—deciding whether you need one, finding one and working with one—although it sometimes includes patronizing advice such as "be patient" with your lawyer and "pay your attorney's bill when it's due."

Plain Language and Glossary　　　　　**Grade: A⁻**

The text and fill-in-the blank documents are written in plain language. *Your Own Living Will* does not include a separate glossary of legal terms, but it does include a list of "definitions" in Chapter 1 that covers the major legal terms found in both living wills and durable powers of attorney for health care.

Easy to Use　　　　　**Grade: B⁻**

Well laid-out and easy to read, *Your Own Living Will* includes plenty of white space, bulleted information and summary reminders in the margins to call the reader's attention to important details. The step-by-step instructions are straightforward, but only cover the book's basic living will form. If you live in a state that has adopted a state-specific form, you are on your own, despite the claim that the directions generally apply to all forms. While it is true that many of the state-specific forms are relatively simple to complete, some states like Minnesota require you to draft a lot of specific language on your own about your health care choices at the end of life.

Red Flags　　　　　**Grade: B⁻**

Although the book includes state laws, references to lawyers and legal research and a few cautions about drafting, *Your Own Living Will* does not highlight many potential

problems or areas of concern such as organ donation
or naming health-care proxies.

Quality of Legal Forms   **Grade: B⁻**
Your Own Living Will instructs you to select a form,
complete it and have it witnessed and notarized. The final
product is a photocopied pre-printed, filled-in form that's
initialed here and there. The addition of a form disk would
allow users to create more professional-looking documents.

Disclaimer
"This publication is designed to provide accurate and authoritative information in regard to the subject matter
covered. It's sold with the understanding that the publisher
is not engaged in rendering legal, accounting, or other professional service. If legal advice or other expert assistance
is required, the services of a competent professional person should be sought."

Overall   **Grade: B**
How to Write Your Own Living Will shows you how
to write a legally valid living will, and at $9.95 is a great
buy for a good book.

                                    Recommended.

Do-It-Yourself Kit: Living Will &
Power of Attorney for Health Care

E-Z Legal Forms, Deerfield Beach, Florida, 1994
Form Kit, $21.95
(954) 480-8933

Not Recommended

Do-It-Yourself Kit: Living Will & Power of Attorney for Health Care includes a 17-page instruction booklet, step-by-step instructions and forms for preparing a living will in all 50 states and the District of Columbia. It also includes a Power of Attorney for Health Care form that is valid for about a dozen states, and asks residents of the remaining states to send in for a free power of attorney form specific to their state. This kit includes other fill-in-the-blank forms (e.g. funeral requests, personal information) and a brief glossary.

Accuracy   **Grade: F**
> *Living Will & Power of Attorney* provides a very basic and cursory discussion about living wills and durable powers of attorney for health care. Since the kit was published in 1994, many states have now adopted specific forms and others have changed their forms, so much of the information in this product is out of date, and should not be used.

Comprehensiveness   **Grade: D**
> *Living Will & Power of Attorney* provides only a "bare bones" explanation of living wills and powers of attorney.

Plain Language and Glossary   **Grade: D**
> The text and fill-in-the-blank documents are generally written in plain language. The kit includes a short glossary,

but omits terms that are used in the forms, such as attorney-in-fact, principal and agent.

Easy to Use   **Grade: C**
Living Will & Power of Attorney is easy to understand and use, but lacks details. The step-by-step instructions are extremely brief (about a page) and do not explain the differences in the state specific forms.

Red Flags   **Grade: F**
The booklet does not use red flags, cite specific state laws or alert you to possible problem areas.

Quality of Legal Forms   **Grade: D**
Living Will & Power of Attorney instructs you to select a form, complete it and have it witnessed and notarized. The final product is a photocopied pre-printed, filled-in form that's initialed here and there.

Disclaimer
"It is understood that by using this legal kit you are acting as your own attorney. Accordingly, the publisher, author and retailer shall have neither liability nor responsibility to any party for any loss or damage caused or alleged to be caused by use of this kit. This kit is sold with the understanding that the publisher, author and retailer are not engaged in rendering legal services. If legal services or other expert assistance are required, the services of a competent professional should be sought."

Overall   **Grade: D**
At $21.95, ***Do-It-Yourself Kit: Living Will & Power of Attorney for Health Care*** contains some good forms and guidance on dealing with end-of-life decisions, but it is outdated and can be dangerous to consumers who rely upon it.

Not Recommended.

Recommended Reading

The Quick & Legal Will Book
by Denis Clifford, Nolo Press, 1996, 240 pages, $15.95
Nolo's Law Form Kit: Wills
by Denis Clifford and Lisa Goldoftas, Nolo Press, 112 pages, 1998, $14.95

Both of these publications provide sound information on writing a simple, no-frills will for the 50-and-under crowd (or more specifically, those who own property valued under the federal estate tax limit). Various wills for single and married individuals, with or without children, are also included. The wills are valid for every state but Louisiana. The step-by-step instructions in each are easy to follow, but require you to create a draft that will need to be typed before being signed and witnessed.

Understanding Living Trusts: How You Can Avoid Probate,
Save Taxes and Enjoy Peace of Mind
by Vickie and Jim Schumacher, Schumacher Publishing, 1997, 266 pages, $24.95

Written by a husband-and-wife team, this reference book offers a comprehensive discussion of revocable living trusts. Loads of good information is included about the kinds of trusts, tax implications of creating a trust, and what to do before and after a trust has been created. There's also very good advice about shopping for a lawyer and suggestions on where to find one, including a referral network created by the authors.

The Living Trust Workbook
by Robert A. Esperti and Renno L. Peterson, Penguin Books, 1995, 319 pages,
$18.95

Designed to be used by those who feel their current estate plan is incomplete, or as a reference for a do-it-yourself living trust kit, *Living Trust Workbook* provides detailed explanations about how a living trust works and how to set one up properly. It includes charts, checklists, sample forms, and worksheets with instructions on how to use them.

The Living Trust
by Henry W. Abts III, Contemporary Books, 1997, 359 pages, $24.95

This reference book on living trusts provides detailed information on probate, estate planning options and especially the living trust. It discusses the formation of a living trust, with many worksheets and samples to help you work with a professional to create one. It also contains an extensive Question and Answer style appendix that covers the most common problems.

7

SMALL BUSINESS

If piled together, the legal forms you need to start and run a small business would be a small mountain. Every day, small business owners use business contracts, bills of sale, real estate leases, promissory and installment notes, receipts and releases, loan documents, collection notices, consulting agreements, confidentiality agreements, partnership agreements, shareholders' agreements, independent contractor agreements, employee performance evaluations—the list could fill this page and many more. Some of these documents are simple and easy to use, others are complex, but do you need to hire a lawyer or learn to speak legalese to use them?

With the products available today, ordinary small business people have the power to do it themselves. Large selections of small-business legal forms are now available from your neighborhood bookstore in publications that offer scores of the documents and letters that businesses use every day. In addition, many of the same publications include a computer disk so you can easily add your information, make changes to your documents and print them.

Most of the publications are written by attorneys and are valid in all 50 states and the District of Columbia. This is possible because the Uniform Commercial Code has standardized business transactions across the country. Although you need to add information about your business to any form, a lawyer is no longer needed to draft the forms and complete them for you. You can do it yourself and use the money you would have spent on legal fees to improve your small business.

The products we review are excellent examples of the options available to the small business owner. There are books with printed forms that also include computer disks, loose-leaf collections of hard copy forms, and CD-ROM software for your computer that interviews you and completes your document at the same time. For most day-in-day-out legal needs, one of these self-help products will fill the bill for most small business owners.

Overall, Kiplinger's *Small Business Attorney*, a comprehensive resource for small businesses, and *Small Business Legal Pro 3* from Nolo Press, stand out and are HALT Do-it-Yourself Best Buys.

Kiplinger's Small Business Attorney
Multimedia Edition
Block Financial Corporation
Kansas City, Missouri, 1998
CD-ROM Software for Windows and Mac, $49.95
(800) 813-7940

HALT
Do-it-Yourself
Best Buy

Kiplinger's Small Business Attorney includes 82 business agreements and documents that cover finances, sales and marketing, personnel and employment, sale and purchase of goods, technology, real estate, estate planning, and asset protection. Some of the legal agreements can also be used by individuals, for example the financial, estate planning and family law documents. *Business Law Topics* is a reference tool that covers an additional 60 specific business topics, such as employment-at-will, uniform commercial code and small claims court. The software also provides a section for storing information about your business that is used to create legal documents, a document editor for saved documents, and a help button for answers to commonly asked questions about how to use the program.

Accuracy   **Grade: A**
Small Business Attorney provides thorough, accurate and complete information on the major areas of legal concern to small businesses, as well as a comprehensive selection of the most commonly used forms.

Comprehensiveness   **Grade: A**
Small Business Attorney is truly a comprehensive resource tool for small business owners with its 82 business agreements and documents, plus a general reference book entitled *Business Law Topics*. None of the estate planning documents, however, specifically address leaving a business to other family members.

Plain Language and Glossary   **Grade: B⁺**

The text in *Business Law Topics* and the individual document descriptions is written in plain language, and is easy to understand. The business forms frequently use boilerplate legal language that is not explained anywhere in the program. For example, "... I hereby waive and disclaim any express or implied covenants...." To be sure you understand the agreement you're creating, it's best to complete it with a legal dictionary in hand. Missing from the program, but included in ***Kiplinger's Home Legal Advisor***, is a dictionary of legal terms. Given the legalese included in some of the legal forms, adding a glossary or dictionary would substantially improve this product.

Easy to Use   **Grade: A**

The program is easy to install and use. You move through different files through clearly marked buttons and links.

To select a business document, you double click on its name from the Create New Document listing of 82 documents. A brief description of the document immediately appears. If, after reading that description, you decide you want to see the actual document, you double click on its name. Red text in the document indicates a place where you need to make a decision (for example, filling in the amount of money owed to you in a promissory note). If you click on the red text, step-by-step instructions on exactly what you need to do appear. Green text, if clicked, provides a more extensive plain-language discussion of that particular clause, and blue text indicates areas you have already completed.

A nice feature is User Data. This allows you to enter information about your business, (e.g. name, place of incorporation, address, phone numbers), and then easily export that information into new legal forms. At other decision points where you may have to draft language, you are given sample language that can automatically be added to your document and edited to fit your circumstances. The program also includes the names and addresses of commonly contacted businesses (like credit bureaus). All you have to do is select the company you want to contact from a list that appears on your screen, and the program dsiplays its current mailing address.

Red Flags **Grade: B**
Small Business Attorney includes warnings about when state law varies, when forms should be reviewed by lawyers, or when additional resources should be consulted, but you have to go hunting for them.

Quality of Legal Forms **Grade: A⁻**
Small Business Attorney allows you to produce great looking, if legalese-filled, documents.

Disclaimer
"The user acknowledges that Block Financial Corporation, The Kiplinger Washington Editors, Inc., and Teneron Corporation do not practice law or provide professional services and are not rendering such professional services with regard to the program. The user acknowledges that laws vary from state to state and change over time. The final documents should be reviewed by a lawyer before use. When a document is to be negotiated with another party, the user should consult an attorney prior to the start of negotiations. In the event any provisions of the Terms of Use are determined to be void or not enforceable, the remaining provisions shall continue in effect."

Overall **Grade: A**
Kiplinger's Small Business Attorney is a very sophisticated product for small business owners that could be improved with the addition of a law dictionary and forms that read a little less like the boilerplate in the form books lawyers use. The estate planning section is useful, but business owners, especially those who want to keep the

business in their family after their death, will need more elaborate estate planning documents than the ones provided here. At $49.95, *Kiplinger's Small Business Attorney* is an exceptional value for any small business.

HALT
Do-it-Yourself
Best Buy

Small Business Legal Pro 3
Nolo Press, Berkeley, California, 1997
CD-ROM Software for Windows and Mac, $79.95
(800) 992-6656

HALT
Do-it-Yourself
Best Buy

Small Business Legal Pro 3 is an electronic reference library containing the full text of six self-help legal titles: *The Legal Guide for Starting and Running a Small Business*, Volumes 1 and 2, *Tax Savvy for Small Business, The Employer's Legal Handbook, Everybody's Guide to Small Claims Court* and *Marketing Without Advertising*. The CD-ROM also includes 120 legal forms, letters and worksheets, a searchable text and index, links to Nolo's legal encyclopedia, and demos for several other Nolo products.

The 120 forms, letters and worksheets found in the various books cover virtually all the major legal needs of business owners, and are compiled for easy access under a Legal Forms for Small Businesses button on the initial screen. If you know what form you need, you can go to it easily. Otherwise, you can learn more about the individual forms and how they're used by reading the detailed discussion in this product.

Accuracy   **Grade: A⁻**

All of the books offered in *Small Business Legal Pro* offer up-to-date and accurate information on various aspects of business law. The only publication slightly out of date is the 1995 edition of *Everybody's Guide to Small Claims Court* included on the CD-ROM. Readers can visit Nolo's web site for updates and new editions.

Comprehensiveness   **Grade: A⁺**

There's a wealth of information on this CD-ROM on

every aspect of small business ownership, from devising a business plan to applying for a business loan, from marketing your product or service to hiring employees, and from resolving disputes to paying your taxes.

Plain Language and Glossary   **Grade: B⁺**
Legalese is used only when necessary and is always explained in the text. A separate glossary of terms is only included in *Tax Savvy for Small Business,* and would be a useful improvement in the other titles included in this package.

Easy to Use   **Grade: A**
Installing and using **Small Business Legal Pro** is easy. Once installed, clearly marked icons take you to the six books included on the CD-ROM, a useful set of instructions for first-time users, a search engine, and a giant searchable index for all six books. Multi-level tables of contents exist for each book, so that you can learn not only what chapters are in a book, but what topics are discussed within each chapter before opening it. Within each chapter you'll find links that allow you to move between related material in the book easily and quickly.

The software is not interactive like Nolo's **WillMaker.** In fact, since this software pulls information from books, the instructions for filling out the forms assume you're reading a book. The authors explain this problem and how to deal with it. For example, you're instructed to ignore text that asked you to "check" which optional clause you want, and instead delete extraneous clause material with your word processor.

Red Flags   **Grade: A**
Areas that warrant special attention are flagged with special icons. Readers are told when local rules may vary, when they need to contact a lawyer, and when other resources should be consulted.

Quality of Legal Forms   **Grade: A**
Small Business Legal Pro includes legal forms, work-sheets and sample letters that can be edited to fit your particular circumstances. The quality of the final document depends greatly on the person creating it, but in general Nolo's directions for filling out forms are thorough, easy to follow, and should produce professional looking documents.

Disclaimer
"We've done our best to give you useful and accurate information in this book. But laws and procedures change frequently and are subject to differing interpretations. If you want legal advice backed by a guarantee, see a lawyer. If you use this book, it's your responsibility to make sure that the facts and general advice contained in it are applicable to your situation."

Overall   **Grade: A**
Small Business Legal Pro 3.0 includes six extremely well-written, easy to understand and thorough books in easy-to-use software. At $79.95 **Small Business Legal Pro** is an exceptional value for any business owner.

HALT
Do-it-Yourself
Best Buy

BUSINESS LetterWorks
2nd Edition
by Stephen P. Elliott, editor
Round Lake Publishing, Ridgefield, Connecticut, 1993
470 pages, $79.95
(203) 438-5255

Recommended

BUSINESS Letter Works includes 400 business letters and memos that can be used as is, or customized to fit your individual circumstances. The authors are communication experts and work for Strategic Communications, a company that teaches executives of Fortune 500 companies how to write more effectively. Topics include customer relations, credit and collections, handling customer complaints, dealing with suppliers, personnel relations, managing your business, internal communications, community service, sales, marketing, advertising, public relations, job searching, and faxes. While most of the model letters are meant to help professionals in their business life, many can be modified for personal use as well, particularly in the area of credit and collections.

Each of the 13 chapters includes introductory material on the business topic covered, such as sales and marketing, and a series of model letters and memos. Under each of the 400 letters and memos are two to three helpful tips. For example, in the form letter entitled Order Received, Being Shipped, the authors stress the following two points: "Express appreciation for the order," and "Detail what was ordered, who is shipping it, and when it is expected to arrive (if possible). Include all relevant purchase order and shipping numbers in case there are problems later."

In some circumstances, the authors also offer a variety of letters on the same issue but in different tones. For example, you can select a collection letter written in a light, moderate or stern tone depending on your style and circumstances.

BUSINESS LetterWorks comes with either a Mac or PC formatted disk. An index by title and an index by subject make it easy to find the right letter or memo.

Accuracy **Grade: A**

BUSINESS LetterWorks provides concise, well-written letters for business use that are easy to understand and modify, and can often be used in place of more formal sounding legal agreements.

Comprehensiveness **Grade: A**

BUSINESS LetterWorks does an excellent job of thoroughly covering major business topics.

Plain Language and Glossary **Grade: B⁺**

Plain language is used in the text and in the sample letters and memoranda. The lack of a glossary of legal terminology is one shortcoming of this product.

Easy to Use **Grade: A⁻**

BUSINESS LetterWorks is easy to read, understand and use. The table of contents and indexes make it easy to find the right letter. The addition of a form disk makes drafting the letter a breeze. If you don't have a computer, you can easily type each letter, since most are only one to two paragraphs long.

Red Flags **Grade: B**

BUSINESS LetterWorks includes warnings about when legal help should be sought and when state law may vary, but the warnings are not highlighted in any obvious way such as boldface, capital lettering, or special icons.

Quality of Legal Forms **Grade: A**

If you follow the tips and use most of the suggested language, you should be able to draft a professional-sounding letter in no time. *BUSINESS LetterWorks* is best for computer users since every letter, even if exactly on point,

has to be customized with the right name, dates and
information about your business.

Disclaimer

"The forms in **BUSINESS *LetterWorks*** are designed
to provide helpful information in regard to the subject matter covered. This product is sold with the understanding
that the publisher is not engaged in rendering legal, accounting or other professional service. If legal advice or
other expert assistance is required, the services of a competent professional person should be sought."

Overall   Grade: A⁻

At $79.95, **BUSINESS *LetterWorks*** is pricey but still
an excellent value. It is a wonderful resource to have on
hand for any business professional. In addition to teach-
ing you how to write better, it imparts good business
practices and communication skills.

Recommended.

The Complete Book of
Small Business Legal Forms
2nd Edition
by Daniel Sitarz
Nova Publishing Company, Carbondale, Illinois, 1997
253 pages, $29.95
(800) 748-1175

Recommended

Small Business Legal Forms is designed to help small business people deal with day-to-day legal problems that arise in the operation of their business. The book contains 18 sections, which cover most business situations–Business Operation Agreements, Contracts, Signatures and Notary Acknowledgments, Powers of Attorney, Releases, Receipts, Leases of Real Estate, Rental of Personal Property, Sale of Personal Property, Sale of Real Estate, Employment Documents, Business Credit Documents, Business Financing Documents, Promissory Notes, Purchase of Goods Documents, Sale of Goods Documents, Collection Documents, and Miscellaneous Business Documents.

Each section of the book features an introduction that provides general background on the relevant law. Each form also includes an explanation of how it should be used. A floppy disk accompanies the book (available in PC and Mac versions) and contains all of the forms and letters in ASCII files that can be used with any word processor.

Accuracy   **Grade: B**

Small Business Legal Forms provides accurate, but somewhat generic, legal forms for a variety of business situations. It provides some background on the law these forms address.

Comprehensiveness   **Grade: A⁻**

It would be impossible to provide every form or letter required for every small business legal situation. Even so,

Small Business Legal Forms provides most forms and letters that most small businesses will need for most day-to-day situations.

Plain Language and Glossary   **Grade: B⁺**
Small Business Legal Forms avoids almost all legalese and is written in plain language, although legal terminology is used as required in the forms. Although most legal terms are explained in the description of the form, the lack of a glossary is one shortcoming of the product.

Easy to Use   **Grade: B**
Small Business Legal Forms is well-organized by subject. Each chapter has an introduction that discusses general legal principles. Each form has an explanation of when the form should be used and the information required to complete the form, along with definitions of legal terms, attachments that should go with the form, and other forms in the book that should be used in conjunction with it. It is not the easiest product to use, however. The included computer disk allows you to edit the forms on your word processor.

Red Flags   **Grade: C**
Small Business Legal Forms provides no information on state differences. This is not much of a problem with business forms, because most states have adopted the Uniform Commercial Code so standardized forms can be used almost everywhere. Minimal information is provided about possible trouble areas and, for those listed, it is recommended that you see a local attorney.

Quality of Legal Forms   **Grade: B⁺**
Small Business Legal Forms contains 138 legal forms on many topics. The forms in the book are not for actual use because they are not of legal size (too small). Instead you must use the computer disk on your word processor. This allows you to edit, cut, paste and make any other

changes to the form for your situation. This is especially helpful when adding clauses (also included in this product) to a customized document. Otherwise, you should copy the form, fill it out, and re-type the form in its entirety on clean letter-sized paper or on business letterhead.

Disclaimer

"Because of possible unanticipated changes in governing statutes and case law relating to the application of any information contained in this book, the author, publisher, and any and all persons or entities involved in any way in the preparation, publication, sale, or distribution of this book disclaim all responsibility for the legal effects or consequences of any document prepared or action taken in reliance upon information contained in this book. No representations, either express or implied, are made or given regarding the legal consequences of the use of any information contained in this book. Purchasers and persons intending to use this book for the preparation of any legal documents are advised to check specifically on the current applicable laws in any jurisdiction in which they intend the documents to be effective."

Overall   **Grade: B⁺**

For the small businessperson who needs a collection of legal forms that cover most day-to-day business situations, at $29.95 ***The Complete Book of Small Business Legal Forms*** is an excellent value.

Recommended.

The Complete Book of Business
& Legal Forms
by Lynn Ann Frasier
Sourcebooks, Inc., Naperville, Illinois, 1996
268 pages, $18.95
(800) 226-5291

Recommended

The Complete Book of Business & Legal Forms is a
resource of practical business information and ready-to-use
forms and letters for your business. The 40 forms cover
Partnerships, Corporations, Purchase/Sale of a Business, Confidentiality Agreements, Employment Agreements, Business
Relationship Agreements, Promissory Notes, Security Agreements, and Intellectual Property Agreements. The 20 business
letters cover common commercial transactions such as contracts, sales and debt collection. Each chapter of the book
features an introduction that provides some background on the
topic as well as forms and letters. Each form also includes a
description that explains its use. In addition, *Business &
Legal Forms* uses a Legal Audit Questionnaire to make you
aware of legal issues and risks in your business, and an Entrepreneur Questionnaire to help you check your own manage-
ment practices.

Accuracy   **Grade: B⁺**
   Business & Legal Forms provides accurate, but somewhat generic, business forms and letters for a wide variety
   of situations, and general explanations of the laws that apply to businesses.

Comprehensiveness   **Grade: B**
   Business & Legal Forms includes standard business
   forms and letters that most small businesses will need in

common situations, as well as business letters covering credit, collection, contracts and sales issues. Standard government forms are also included, such as intellectual property forms, IRS SS-4–Federal Employer Identification Number, IRS Form 2553–Subchapter S Corporate Election, and suggested forms from the Uniform Commercial Code.

Plain Language and Glossary   **Grade: B**
Business & Legal Forms successfully avoids almost all legalese and is written in plain language. The lack of a glossary of legal terminology is one shortcoming of this product.

Easy to Use   **Grade: B⁻**
Business & Legal Forms is organized by subject, with an introduction to each chapter that generally explains applicable law. Each form has a short description that tells you what the form means, how it applies to you and when you should use it. The forms and letters are generic and are designed to be re-typed with your information on plain paper or company letterhead. Each chapter also has a tips section that offers pointers on drafting, negotiating, entering into agreements, letter writing, and preparing government forms. It does not provide tear-out forms, or forms that can be photocopied. They must be retyped. This is safer, but less convenient.

Red Flags   **Grade: B**
Business & Legal Forms provides some information on state-by-state differences in interpretations of the Uniform Commercial Code. It highlights the states where incorporation requirements are different, and contains an appendix of phone numbers for the incorporation and trademark agencies in all 50 states. Generally, it warns you to obtain legal counsel to review your documents to make sure they comply with state laws.

Quality of Legal Forms   **Grade: B⁻**

Business & Legal Forms contains business forms, business letters and government forms, but the forms in the book are not for actual use and are not perforated. Instead you must re-type the form in its entirety on plain paper, or on business letterhead.

Disclaimer

"This publication is designed to provide accurate and authoritative information in regard to the subject matter covered. It is sold with the understanding that the publisher is not engaged in rendering legal, accounting, or other professional service. If legal advice or other expert assistance is required, the services of a competent professional person should be sought."

Overall   **Grade: B**

For the small business person who would like a collection of business forms and letters that covers most common situations, *The Complete Book of Business & Legal Forms* is a thorough resource that includes a legal audit and entrepreneur questionnaire that can help you improve your business practices. At $18.95, *The Complete Book of Business & Legal Forms* is an excellent value for small businesses.

Recommended.

Good Value

The Most Valuable Business Legal Forms You'll Ever Need
2nd Edition
by James C. Ray
Sourcebooks, Inc., Naperville, Illinois, 1998
165 pages, $19.95
(800) 226-5291

The Most Valuable Business Legal Forms You'll Ever Need includes a general overview of contract law and 50 forms covering a variety of business areas, such as sales agreements, employment agreements, contracts for services, real estate and lease agreements, releases, affidavits, powers of attorney, promissory notes, credit applications, mediation, and arbitration agreements.

Accuracy **Grade: B⁻**

Most Valuable Business Legal Forms provides an accurate, but fairly general overview of contract law, and does not include state-specific citations. Instead the book comments that general principles of contract law apply everywhere, and advises you that "competent legal advice is always desirable."

Comprehensiveness **Grade: C⁺**

Most Valuable Business Legal Forms includes 10 chapters and a set of 50 forms that cover many common business needs. In Chapter 1, after a general discussion of contract law, a sample contract is broken down into its parts and explained. Chapters 2 thru 10 cover employees, independent contractors, powers of attorney, buying, selling and leasing real estate, buying, selling and renting merchandise and equipment, sale and purchase of a business, borrowing and lending money, and avoiding liability and settling disputes.

Each chapter includes a legal explanation and a sample form that has been completed. These examples serve as the step-by-step instructions, so you have to flip back to the chapter that covers each form to be able to use this product. In many forms you must draft critical descriptive language on your own.

Plain Language and Glossary   **Grade: C**
Plain language is used in the text and the forms, although quite a bit of legalese creeps into the forms here and there. The lack of a glossary that defines legal terminology is one shortcoming of this product.

Easy to Use   **Grade: C**
Readers can get a fairly good idea of how to complete the forms provided in this book by reviewing the completed sample forms, but they are not a substitute for good step-by-step instructions. Users are urged to photocopy the forms and type the information needed to complete them. A form disk, which is not included in this product, would allow readers to generate forms more easily and quickly.

Red Flags   **Grade: C**
Most Valuable Business Legal Forms includes some warnings about when legal help should be sought and when state law may vary, but the warnings are not presented in any obvious way, such as boldface, capital lettering or special icons.

Quality of Legal Forms   **Grade: B⁻**
Most Valuable Business Legal Forms includes forms that can be photocopied and completed, but the lack of step-by-step instructions makes it difficult to produce professional looking documents.

Disclaimer
"This publication is designed to provide accurate and authoritative information in regard to the subject matter

covered. It is sold with the understanding that the publisher is not engaged in rendering legal, accounting, or
other professional service. If legal advice or other expert
assistance is required, the services of a competent professional person should be sought."

Overall **Grade: C⁺**

***The Most Valuable Business Legal Forms You'll
Ever Need*** provides a good selection of business forms
and information. At $19.95, it is a good value for experi-
enced business people who have a working knowledge of
commercial law. For those who are new to the do-it-yourself movement, a publication with good step-by-step
instructions is a better choice.

Good Value.

Quicken Business Law Partner 3.0
Parsons Technology, 1998
CD-ROM Software for Mac (tested), and
Windows 3.1/95/NT, $29.95
(800) 779-6000

Good Value

Quicken Business Law Partner 3.0 includes 77 legal documents and a *Document Advisor* that interviews you and provides a report of recommended documents. The software also includes a *Legal Help* feature, where you have two options: *Document Information* and *Ask Arthur Miller*. *Document Information* provides some background on the law, a summary of the document and its uses and links to other summaries that offer complimentary information. *Ask Arthur Miller* provides a talking head video of Harvard Law School Professor Arthur Miller who delivers brief lectures on various legal subjects. The program also provides an *Online* feature that connects you to Parsons Technology, where you can get updates and purchase add-on law dictionaries and legal guides.

Accuracy   **Grade: B**
   Business Law Partner provides accurate, although somewhat generic, legal forms for a variety of business situations that are customized through the interview process. It also discusses the legal topics and individual forms through the *Legal Help* button.

Comprehensiveness   **Grade: C**
   Business Law Partner provides 77 legal documents for use with your small business. Although the forms provided are the ones that are used most often by small business, other products often provide over 100 legal

forms. The 77 forms do cover many of the most common situations a small business will encounter.

Plain Language and Glossary   **Grade: C**
Business Law Partner generally avoids the use of legalese, but legal terminology is frequently used by the forms. All legal terms are explained in the *Document Information* mechanism. Although *Document Information* and *Ask Arthur Miller* provide some help in understanding legal terminology, they are not an adequate substitute for a complete glossary or a full law dictionary. Parson's offers to sell you the *Plain Language Law Dictionary* and the *American Bar Association Family Legal Guide* as additional purchase add-ons.

Easy to Use   **Grade: A**
Business Law Partner is extremely easy to use. Installation is a double-click on the install icon and then the simple Mac install procedure, i.e. restart when done. Once installed, the program is easy to navigate and use. Completing a form is easy. Once you select the legal document you wish to use, it will appear on your screen and an interview dialog will appear. By answering the interview questions, the form will be automatically completed on the screen. Two types of help are available during the interview process, *How do I?* and *Legal Help*. *How do I?* answers technical questions on how to do things in the program. *Legal Help* provides legal information on the document you're working on. You can easily export a document to the built-in editor or your word processor if you want to cut, paste or make other edits. A tool bar at the top of the screen provides easy access to functions like printing, saving, spell check and help.

Red Flags   **Grade: C**
Business Law Partner uses its interview and document advisor modules to identify potential problems, but it pro-

vides little information on state differences. This is not
much of a problem with business forms, because most
states have adopted the Uniform Commercial Code, so the
forms should be applicable almost everywhere.

Quality of Legal Forms   **Grade: A**
   Business Law Partner allows you to produce excellent
looking documents.

Disclaimer
   "***Business Law Partner*** is designed to provide information and forms you may find helpful. It is provided to you
with the understanding that Parsons Technology is not
engaged in providing legal advice or other professional
services. It is not intended to replace legal advice and if
legal advice or other expert assistance is required, the services of a competent and qualified lawyer or other
professional should be sought."

Overall   **Grade: C⁺**
   For the small business person who would like a collection
of forms that cover common business situations in an extremely easy-to-use format, at $29.95 ***Quicken Business
Law Partner*** is a good value. The need to purchase a
dictionary as well will come as an annoying surprise, however, to do-it-yourself consumers who expect to get what
they paid for.
                                            Good Value.

Standard Legal Forms and Agreements for Small Business

by Steve Sanderson, editor
Self-Counsel Press, Inc., Bellingham, Washington, 1990
198 pages, $14.95
(800) 663-3007   ***Good Value***

Printed on recycled paper, ***Standard Legal Forms and Agreements for Small Business*** includes over 130 forms covering new businesses, services, employment, buying, selling, collections, credit/debit, leases, assignments, and corporations. Chapters on estate planning and real estate for the small business owner are also included. Each chapter begins with a brief description of the kind of forms you'll find. While some of these descriptions include step-by-step instructions for using the form, others do not.

Accuracy   **Grade: B**

Standard Legal Forms, although published in 1990, still offers sound legal documents that address many of the legal concerns small business owners may have.

Comprehensiveness   **Grade: C**

Over 130 documents are included. While technically accurate, most are written in boilerplate style and offer only one response to a particular business situation. It would be more helpful to have alternative language suggestions for common business occurrences. For example, businesses would lose good customers who, when paying for services, make honest mistakes. The Bad Check Letter threatens collection proceedings if the check isn't replaced within 10 days, and is written in a very confrontational tone. Other documents also use a no-frills business style that can be equally off-putting.

Plain Language and Glossary   **Grade: D**
Formal and legalistic language is used in most of the book's
forms. The lack of a glossary that explains business legal
terms used, such as *warrants, breach,* and *joint and sever-
ally,* is a major shortcoming in this product.

Easy to Use   **Grade: C**
Standard Legal Forms is well-organized, and the forms
are clearly labeled and easy to find. The author identifies
which forms you might want to retype, and which ones can
be photocopied and then completed. The lack of good
step-by-step instructions means this is not the most user-
friendly product.

Red Flags   **Grade: C**
Standard Legal Forms does include some warnings
when legal help should be sought and when you need to be
particularly careful, but they are not presented in any obvious way, such as boldface, capital lettering or special
icons, nor are they as comprehensive as those used in more
complete publications.

Quality of Legal Forms   **Grade: C**
The lack of a computer disk or CD-ROM with forms makes
it difficult to produce professional-looking documents.
Nevertheless, ***Standard Legal Forms*** includes many
basic forms that can easily be photocopied and completed,
or re-typed.

Disclaimer
"Laws are constantly changing. Every effort is made to
keep this publication as current as possible. However,
neither the editor nor the publisher can accept any responsibility for changes to the law or practice that occur after
the printing of this publication. Please be sure that you

have the most recent edition."

Overall   **Grade: C**

At $14.95, ***Standard Legal Forms*** is a good value as a general reference tool for business owners, but business professionals who want to avoid legal fees by drafting their own documents will be put off by the strident tone of some of the documents and letters as well as the need to re-type forms to produce professional-looking documents.

Good Value.

Business Lawyer

E-Z Legal Software, Deerfield Beach, Florida
CD-ROM and Computer Disk for Windows 3.1/95, $29.95
(954) 840-8933

Not Recommended

Business Lawyer contains 301 legal forms and agreements for various business and personal needs. All of the forms are available on the CD-ROM or floppy disks, and can be used with Windows 3.1/95. No other materials aside from the registration card are included.

Accuracy   **Grade: C⁻**

Business Lawyer provides accurate, but extremely general, legal forms and agreements for a variety of business and personal situations. The forms can be edited before printing.

Comprehensiveness   **Grade: C-**

Business Lawyer contains 301 legal forms and agreements for use with your business or personal matters. They are arranged in the following categories—Basic Agreements, Loans & Borrowing, Employment, Credit & Collection, Buying & Selling, Leases & Tenancies, Transfers & Assignments, Personal & Family, Real Estate, Business, and Other Legal Forms. Although the program is called **Business Lawyer**, it also includes many forms for personal use, such as cohabitation agreements, child guardianships, last will & testament, organ donation and premarital agreements.

The large number of forms in **Business Lawyer** cover many common business needs, but their content is very generic. Even though each form attempts to cover a wide variety of situations, no background on the legal topics is provided, and it often leaves you in the dark regarding the legal concepts behind these documents.

Plain Language and Glossary **Grade: F**
The forms in **Business Lawyer** tend to be very generic and contain boilerplate legalese. After filling out some of the forms, you may be hard pressed to understand them. The lack of a glossary explaining the legal jargon is a major shortcoming in this product.

Easy to Use **Grade: F**
Business Lawyer is very easy to install using a standard "setup" utility. This is where the ease ends, however. A screen greets you that allows you to click on a category—Basic Agreements, Loans & Borrowing, Employment, Credit & Collection, Buying & Selling, Leases & Tenancies, Transfers & Assignments, Personal & Family, Real Estate, Business and Other Legal Forms—which displays a list of the forms. Only the briefest description of the form is displayed, which provides little information beyond the title of the document.

After selecting a form, an interactive interface is used to collect the needed information which is automatically placed in the form. This interface is very slow—even on a Pentium, although the program is supposed to run on a 486 or higher—and feels clunky and rough. After you enter your information, you may edit or print your document. No written instructions are included with the product and no help with the legal concepts or terminology is provided. In many ways, you are simply left to your own devices.

Red Flags **Grade: F**
Business Lawyer does not point out possible trouble areas or possible differences in state law.

Quality of Legal Forms **Grade: C⁻**
Business Lawyer contains 301 legal forms and agree-

ments that produce excellent-looking documents. Unless you are a lawyer or have extensive experience dealing with legalese, however, you may not be able to understand the documents it creates.

Disclaimer

"It is understood that by using this software you are acting as your own attorney. Accordingly, the publisher, author, retailer and distributor shall have neither liability nor responsibility to any person or entity with respect to loss or damage caused or alleged to be caused directly or indirectly by the use of the information contained in this software. In no event shall our liability exceed the purchase price of this software. Use of the software constitutes acceptance of these terms."

Overall   **Grade: D**

For $29.95, ***Business Lawyer*** is not for do-it-yourself consumers who do not have an extensive legal background. The lack of both instruction and explanations of legal concepts makes it potentially dangerous for most consumers.

Not Recommended.

APPENDICES

SELF-HELP PUBLISHERS

The following is a list of publishers that produce do-it-yourself and self-help legal materials. Some offer state-specific titles, while others produce both state-specific and national titles. For more information on what a publisher produces, call or write for a catalog.

Allworth Press
10 E. 23rd St., Ste. 210
New York, NY 10010
(800) 491-2808

Avery Publishing Co.
120 Old Broadway
Garden City Park, NY 11040
(516) 741-2155

Barron's Educational Series
250 Wireless Blvd.
Hauppauge, NY 11788
(800) 645-3467

Bell Springs Publishing
P.O. Box 1240
Willits, CA 95490
(800) 515-8050

Block Financial Corp.
4435 Main St.
Kansas City, MO 64111
(800) 813-7940

Boardroom Classics
P.O. Box 11014
Des Moines, IA 50336
(800) 678-5835

Commerce Clearinghouse
21250 Hawthorne Blvd.
Torrance, CA 90503
(800) 457-7639

BNA Books
P.O. Box 7814
Edison, NJ 08818
(800) 457-7639

Dearborn Financial
155 N. Wacker Dr.
Chicago, IL 60606
(312) 836-4400

E-Z Legal Forms, Inc.
384 S. Military Trail
Deerfield Beach, FL 33442
(954) 480-8933

Easy Wills Publishing
1336 Saddleridge Dr.
Orlando, FL 32835
(888) 891-1578

F.B. Rothman & Co.
10368 W. Centennial Rd.
Litttleton, CO 80127
(800) 457-1986

Garrett Publishing, Inc.
384 S. Military Trail
Deerfield Beach, FL 33442
(954) 480-8543

Grand River Press
P.O. Box 1342
E. Lansing, MI 48823
(517) 332-8181

Homestead Publishing
4455 Torrance Blvd., Ste. 220
Torrance, CA 90503-4392
(213) 214-3559

Horizon Publishers
50 South - 500 West
Bountiful, UT 84010
(800) 453-0812

Intuit, Inc.
2650 E. Elvira Rd.
Tucson, AZ 85706-7180
(650) 922-3538

JIAN, Inc.
1975 W. El Camino Real
Mountain View, CA 94040
(800) 346-5426

John Wiley and Sons
605 3rd Ave.
New York, NY 10158
(800) 225-5945

Legal Aid Forms, Inc.
3605 N. 7th Ave., Ste. 100
Phoenix, AZ 85013
(602) 252-8888

Legisoft
3430 Noriega
San Francisco, CA 94122
(415) 566-9136

LK Enterprises
1961 Route One Rd.
Marietta, TX 75566
(903) 825-6223

Longmeadow Press
201 High Ridge Rd.
Stamford, CT 06904
(203) 352-2648

Macmillan Publishing
201 W. 103rd St.
Indianapolis, IN 46290
(800) 716-0044

MECA Software, LLC
115 Corporate Dr.
Trumbull, CT 06611
(203) 452-2600

Merritt Publishing
401 Wilshire Blvd., Ste. 800
Santa Monica, CA 90401-1430
(800) 638-7597

Nolo Press
950 Parker St.
Berkeley, CA 94710
(800) 992-6656

Nova Publishing Co.
1103 W. College St.
Carbondale, IL 62901
(800) 748-1175

NTC Contemporary
4255 Touhy Ave.
Lincolnwood, IL 60646
(312) 782-9181

Oceana Group
75 Main St.
Dobbs Ferry, NY 10522
(800) 831-0758

Parsons Technology
1700 Progress Dr., Box 100
Hiawatha, IA 52233-0100
(800) 779-6000

Penguin Putnam
120 Woodbine St.
Bergenfield, NJ 07621-0120
(800) 526-0275

Prometheus Books
59 John Glenn Dr.
Amherst, NY 14228-2197
(716) 691-0137

ProSe Associates
9889 S. Spring Hill Dr.
Highlands Ranch, CO 80126
(303) 470-9597

PSI Research
300 N. Valley Dr.
Grants Pass, OR 97526
(800) 228-2275

Round Lake Publishing
31 Barley Ave.
Ridgefield, CT 06877
(203) 438-5255

Schumacher Publishing
3000 Ocean Park Blvd.
Santa Monica, CA 90405
(800) 728-2665, ext. 41

Self-Counsel Press, Inc.
1704 N. State St.
Bellingham, WA 98225
(800) 663-3007

SJT Enterprises, Inc.
11311 Franklin Ave.
Cleveland, OH 44102
(800) 326-7419

Sourcebooks, Inc.
P.O. Box 372
Naperville, IL 60566
(800) 226-5291

The Forms Man, Inc.
10 Darius Ct.
Dix Hills, NY 11746
(516) 242-0009

Unabridged Software
3355 W. Alabama, 3rd Fl.
Houston, TX 77098
(713) 552-0490

Van O'Steen & Partners
3605 N. 7th Ave., Ste. 100
Phoenix, AZ 85013
(602) 252-8888

BIBLIOGRAPHY

The following bibliography includes self-help and do-it-yourself products organized by legal topic. While comprehensive, it is not an exhaustive list of what's available, since new titles are always being released. For the latest products available, please check Books-in-Print or ask at your local bookstore.

Bankruptcy

The Bankruptcy Kit, by John Ventura. Dearborn Financial Publishing, Inc., 155 N. Wacker Dr., Chicago, IL 60606-1719. 1996. $19.95. 214 pages.
(See profile, Chapter 5.)

Bankruptcy Law for the Individual Debtor, by Margaret C. Jasper. Oceana Publications, Inc., 75 Main St., Dobbs Ferry, NY 10522. 1997. $22.50. 86 pages.
Provides a general discussion of bankruptcy law in the United States and the procedure an individual must follow to file a bankruptcy petition. Appendices include sample forms, state laws and a glossary of terms.

Bankruptcy: Step-by-Step, by James John Jurinski. Barron's Educational Series, Inc., 250 Wireless Blvd., Hauppauge, NY 11788. 1996. $14.95. 225 pages.
(See profile, Chapter 5.)

Chapter 13 Bankruptcy: Repay Your Debts, by Robin Leonard. Nolo Press, 950 Parker St., Berkeley, CA 94710. 1998. $29.95. 368 pages.
(See profile, Chapter 5.)

Debt Free: The National Bankruptcy Kit, by Daniel Sitarz. Nova Publishing Co., 1103 W. College St., Carbondale, IL 62901. 1995 (1st Ed.). $17.95. 253 pages.
(See profile, Chapter 5.)

Do-It-Yourself Chapter 7 Bankruptcy Kit. SJT Enterprises, Inc., 11311 Franklin Ave., Cleveland, OH 44102. 1997. $24.95. Form Kit.
(See profile, Chapter 5.)

Do-It-Yourself Kit: Bankruptcy. E-Z Legal Forms, Inc., 384 S. Military Trail, Deerfield Beach, FL 33442. 1991. $21.95. Form Kit.
(See profile, Chapter 5.)

How to File for Bankruptcy, by Stephen Elias, Albin Renauer, and Robin Leonard. Nolo Press, 950 Parker St., Berkeley, CA 94710. 1998 (7th Ed.). $26.95. 475 pages.
(See profile, Chapter 5.)

How to File Your Own Bankruptcy (or How to Avoid It), by Edward A. Haman. Sourcebooks, Inc., P.O. Box 372, Naperville, IL 60566. 1998 (4th Ed.). $19.95. 200 pages.
(See profile, Chapter 5.)

Nolo's Law Form Kit: Personal Bankruptcy, by Stephen Elias, Albin Renauer, Robin Leonard and Lisa Goldoftas. Nolo Press, 950 Parker St., Berkeley, CA 94710. 1997. $14.95. 169 pages. (See profile, Chapter 5.)

Credit/Debtor Rights

The Budget Kit: The Common Cent$ Money Management Workbook, by Judy Lawrence. Dearborn Financial Publishing, Inc., 155 N. Wacker Dr., Chicago, IL 60606-1719. 1997 (2nd Ed.). $15.95. 113 pages.
Explains how to plan and manage your finances and provides worksheets for developing a budget and sticking to it.

Credit Repair, by Robin Leonard. Nolo Press, 950 Parker St., Berkeley, CA 94710. 1997 (2nd Ed.). $15.95. 232 pages.
Explains what you need to do to improve bad credit. Includes 30 forms and form letters for improving your credit.

Debtors' Rights, by Gudrun Maria Nickel. Sourcebooks, Inc., P.O. Box 372, Naperville, IL 60566. 1998 (3rd Ed.). $12.95. 229 pages.
Explains the types of actions creditors can take against you for non-payment and your possible defenses. Includes information about your rights under federal law regarding collection agencies and credit reporting.

Guaranteed Credit, by Arnold S. Goldstein. Garrett Publishing, Inc., 384 S. Military Trail, Deerfield Beach, FL 33442. 1996. $24.95. 293 pages.
Step-by-step information on how to repair, restore and rebuild your credit. Includes sample credit reports and letters, and federal legislation regarding credit.

Estate Planning

8 Ways to Avoid Probate, by Mary Randolph. Nolo Press, 950
   Parker St., Berkeley, CA 94710. 1998. $15.95. 216 pages.
   A part of Nolo's Quick & Legal Series, this book teaches you
   eight different ways to pass property outside of probate.

Avoid Probate: Make Your Own Living Trust, by Denis Clifford.
   Nolo Press, 950 Parker St., Berkeley, CA 94710. 1998. $24.95.
   336 pages.
   (See profile, Chapter 6.)

Complete Estate Planning Kit. SJT Enterprises, Inc., 11311
   Franklin Ave., Cleveland, OH 44102. 1997. $24.95. Form Kit.
   Provides information and forms for completing a will, living will,
   and living trust. Also includes a workbook titled *Estate Planner,* to
   organize all personal, financial and other relevant information.

Do-It-Yourself Kit: Last Will and Testament. E-Z Legal Forms,
   Inc., 384 S. Military Trail, Deerfield Beach, FL 33442. 1995.
   $21.95. Form Kit.
   (See profile, Chapter 6.)

Do-It-Yourself Kit: Living Trust. E-Z Legal Forms, Inc., 384 S.
   Military Trail, Deerfield Beach, FL 33442. 1995. $18.95. Form Kit.
   (See profile, Chapter 6.)

Do-It-Yourself Kit: Living Trust Agreement. SJT Enterprises, Inc.,
   11311 Franklin Ave., Cleveland, OH 44102. 1996. $14.95.
   Form Kit.
   (See profile, Chapter 6.)

*Do-It-Yourself Kit: Living Will & Power of Attorney for
   Healthcare.* E-Z Legal Forms, Inc., 384 S. Military Trail,
   Deerfield Beach, FL 33442. 1995. $21.95. Form Kit.
   (See profile, Chapter 6.)

The Financial Power of Attorney Workbook, by Shae Irving. Nolo Press, 950 Parker St., Berkeley, CA 94710. 1997. $24.95. 250 pages with disk.
(See profile, Chapter 6).

Encyclopedia of Estate Planning, by Robert S. Holzman and John J. Tuozzolo. Boardroom Classics, 55 Railroad Ave., Greenwich, CT 06830. 1998. $29.95. 310 pages.
A reference tool that covers all the major estate planning tools including wills, trusts, gifts to minors, life insurance, anuities and more.

Estate Planning, by Martin M. Shenkman. Barron's Educational Series, Inc., 250 Wireless Blvd., Hauppauge, NY 11788. 1997. $14.95. 244 pages.
A book that takes you through the legal and practical details of planning an estate, protecting assets and minimize probate costs.

Estate Planning, by Harry G. Turner. Merritt Professional Publishing, 1661 9th St., Santa Monica, CA 90406. 1996. $49.95. 300 pages.
Describes the estate planning process, including wills, gifts, trusts, insurance, and other investment products.

Estate Planning for the 1990s, by Vijay Fadia. Homestead Publishing Co. Inc., 21707 Hawthorne Blvd., Suite 204, Torrance, CA 90503. 1995. $39.95. 411 pages.
A reference guide to estate planning. Covers wills, trusts, life insurance, lifetime gifts, annuities and more.

How to Make Your Own Will, by Mark Warda. Sourcebooks, Inc., P.O. Box 372, Naperville, IL 60566. 1998. $12.95. 126 pages.
(See profile, Chapter 6.)

How to Write Your Own Living Will, by Edward A. Haman.
Sourcebooks, Inc., P.O. Box 372, Naperville, IL 60566. 1997.
$9.95. 148 pages.
(See profile, Chapter 6.)

How to Write Your Own Will, by Edward A. Haman.
Sourcebooks, Inc., P.O. Box 372, Naperville, IL 60566. 1997.
$9.95. 144 pages.
(See profile, Chapter 6.)

Last Will and Testament. E-Z Legal Software, 384 S. Military Trail,
Deerfield Beach, FL 33442. 1998. $14.95 Form Kit.
(See profile, Chapter 6.)

Living Trust. E-Z Legal Software, 384 S. Military Trail, Deerfield
Beach, FL 33442. 1998. $29.95. Software.
(See profile, Chapter 6.)

Living Trust Maker 2.0. Nolo Press, 950 Parker St., Berkeley, CA
94710. 1998. $79.95. Software.
(See profile, Chapter 6.)

Living Trust Builder. JIAN, 1975 W. El Camino Real, Suite 301,
Mountain View, CA 94040-2218. 1995. $49.00. Software.
(See profile, Chapter 6.)

The Living Trust, by Henry W. Abts, III. NTC/Contemporary
Books, Inc., 4255 W. Touhy Ave., Lincolnwood, IL 60646-1975.
1997. $24.95. 359 pages.
(See profile, Chapter 6.)

The Living Trust: A Cure for the Agony of Probate, by Vijay Fadia.
Homestead Publishing Co., 21707 Hawthrone Blvd., Suite 204,
Torrance, CA 90503. 1996. $39.95. 193 pages.
(See profile, Chapter 6.)

Living Trusts, by Doug H. Moy. John Wiley & Sons, Inc., 605 3rd Ave., New York, NY 10158-0012. 1997. $39.95. 407 pages. (See profile, Chapter 6.)

Living Trusts and Simple Ways to Avoid Probate, by Karen Ann Rolcik. Sourcebooks, Inc., P.O. Box 372, Naperville, IL 60566. 1998 (2nd Ed). $19.95. 159 pages. (See profile, Chapter 6.)

Nolo's Law Form Kit: Wills, by Denis Clifford and Lisa Goldoftes. Nolo Press, 950 Parker St., Berkeley, CA 94710. 1998. $14.95. 112 pages. (See profile, Chapter 6.)

Nolo's Will Book, by Denis Clifford. Nolo Press, 950 Parker St., Berkeley, CA 94710. 1997 (3rd Ed.). $29.95. 228 pages with disk. (See profile, Chapter 6.)

Plan Your Estate, by Denis Clifford and Cora Jordan. Nolo Press, 950 Parker St., Berkeley, CA 94710. 1998 (4th Ed.). $24.95. 416 pages. (See profile, Chapter 6.)

Prepare Your Own Will: The National Will Kit, by Daniel Sitarz. Nova Publishing Co., 1103 W. College St., Carbondale, IL 62901. 1996 (4th Ed). $27.95. 246 pages with disk. (See profile, Chapter 6.)

Quicken Estate Planner. Parsons Technology, P.O. Box 100, Hiawatha, IA 52233-0100. 1998. $29.95. Software. Program included in Quicken's Family Lawyer. (See profile, Chapter 1.)

The Quick & Legal Will Book, by Denis Clifford. Nolo Press, 950
   Parker St., Berkeley, CA 94710. 1996. $15.95. 240 pages.
   (See profile, Chapter 6.)

The Women's Estate Planning Guide, by Zoe M. Hicks. NTC/
   Contemporary Books, Inc., 4255 W. Touhy Ave., Lincolnwood,
   IL 60646-1975. 1998. $19.95. 279 pages.
   Estate planning advice for women. Information on wills, trusts,
   guardianships, taxes and more.

Thy Will Be Done, Eugene J. Daly. Prometheus Books, 59 John
   Glenn Dr., Amherst, NY 14228-2197. 1994 (2nd Ed.). $17.95.
   234 pages.
   Primarily a guide for writing your will but also offers information on probate, distribution of assets, trusts and ways to cut
   estate taxes.

Understanding Living Trusts, by Vickie and Jim Schumacher.
   Schumacher Publishing, P.O. Box 64395, Los Angeles, CA
   90064-9748. 1996 (4th Ed). $24.95. 266 pages.
   (See profile, Chapter 6.)

WillMaker 6.0/7.0. Nolo Press, 950 Parker St., Berkeley, CA
   94710. 1998. $69.95. Software.
   (See profile, Chapter 6.)

Your Living Trust and Estate Plan, by Harvey J. Platt. Allworth
   Press, Inc., 10 E. 23rd St., New York, NY 10010. 1995. $14.95.
   255 pages.
   In addition to covering traditional estate planning topics this book
   addresses estate planning for the HIV positive, retirement benefits
   and planning for children with special needs.

Family Law

A Legal Guide for Lesbian and Gay Couples, by Hayden Curry,
Denis Clifford and Robin Leonard. Nolo Press, 950 Parker St.,
Berkeley, CA 94710. 1996 (9th Ed.). $24.95. 344 pages.
(See profile, Chapter 2.)

Child Custody: Building Parenting Agreements That Work, by
Mimi E. Lyster. Nolo Press, 950 Parker St., Berkeley, CA
94710. 1997 (2nd Ed.). $24.95. 208 pages.
(See profile, Chapter 2.)

*Divorce & Money: How to Make the Best Financial Decisions
During Divorce*, by Violet Woodhouse, Victoria F. Collins and
M.C. Blakeman. Nolo Press, 950 Parker St., Berkeley, CA
94710. 1998 (3rd Ed.). $26.95. 296 pages.
Strategies for getting through a divorce without going broke.
Divorce & Money provides you with easy-to-use worksheets,
charts, formulas and tables.

Divorce Yourself: The National No-Fault Divorce Kit, by Daniel
Sitarz. Nova Publishing Co., 1103 W. College St., Carbondale,
IL 62901. 1996. $24.95. 333 pages.
(See profile, Chapter 2.)

Do-It-Yourself: No-Fault Divorce Kit. SJT Enterprises, Inc., 11311
Franklin Ave., Cleveland, OH 44102. 1998. $24.95. Form Kit.
(See profile, Chapter 2.)

Grandparents' Rights, by Traci Truly. Sphinx Publishing, 1725
Clearwater-Largo Rd., S., Clearwater, FL 34617. 1995. $19.95.
148 pages.
Provides information on the rights of grandparents in visitation
and custody issues. Explains how to take a case through court,
provides state-specific laws and court forms.

How to File Your Own Divorce, by Edward A. Haman.
Sourcebooks, Inc., P.O. Box 372, Naperville, IL 60566. 1998
(3rd Ed.). $19.95. 238 pages.
(See profile, Chapter 2.)

How to Write Your Own Premarital Agreement, by Edward A.
Haman. Sourcebooks, Inc., P.O. Box 372, Naperville, IL 60566.
1998 (2nd Ed.). $19.95. 175 pages.
(See profile, Chapter 2.)

The Living Together Kit: A Legal Guide for Unmarried Couples, by
Toni Ihara & Ralph Warner. Nolo Press, 950 Parker St., Berke-
ley, CA 94710. 1997 (8th Ed.). $24.95. 245 pages.
(See profile, Chapter 2.)

Nolo's Pocket Guide to Family & Divorce Law, by Robin Leonard
and Stephen Elias. Nolo Press, 950 Parker St., Berkeley, CA
94710. 1996 (4th Ed.). $14.95. 187 pages.
Resource on family law–marriage, divorce, adoption, custody,
surrogracy, living together and more.

Legal Encyclopedias
The 21st Century Family Legal Guide, Joseph W. Mierzwa. ProSe
Associates, Inc., P.O. Box 4333, Highlands Ranch, CO 80126.
1994. $19.95. 451 pages.
Provides general legal information on a variety of topics including
family law, property ownership, money, insurance, tax law and
more. State and local resources included.

301 Legal Forms and Agreements. E-Z Legal Forms, Inc., 384 S.
Military Trail, Deerfield Beach, FL 33442. 1993. $24.95. 282
pages.
(See profile, Chapter 1.)

The Complete Book of Personal Legal Forms, by Daniel Sitarz.
    Nova Publishing, 1103 W. College St., Carbondale, IL 62901.
    1997. 253 pages.
    (See profile, Chapter 1.)

Do-It-Yourself Assorted Legal Forms. SJT Enterprises, Inc., 11311
    Franklin Ave., Cleveland, OH 44102. 1997. $9.95. Form Kit.
    (See profile, Chapter 1.)

Kiplinger's Home Legal Advisor '98. Block Financial Corporation,
    4435 Main St., Kansas City, MO 64111. 1998 (Deluxe Ed.).
    $49.95. Software.
    (See profile, Chapter 1.)

*Law for the Layperson: An Annotated Bibliography of Self-Help
    Law Books,* by Jean Sinclair McKnight. F.B. Rothman and Co.,
    10368 W. Centennial Rd., Littleton, CO 80127. 1977. $47.50.
    228 pages.
    A compliation of self-help law books, both national and state
    specific. Includes author and title index.

The Legal Forms Kit, by Vijay Fadia. Homestead Publishing Co.,
    23844 Hawthorne Blvd., Suite 200, Torrance, CA 90505. 1995.
    $39.95. 394 pages.
    (See profile, Chapter 1.)

LEGAL LetterWorks, by Charles B. Chernofsky and Griffith G.
    deNoyelles, Jr. Round Lake Publishing, 31 Bailey Ave.,
    Ridgefield, CT 06877. 1998. $79.95. 558 pages.
    (See profile, Chapter 1.)

Legal-Wise: Self-Help Legal Guide for Everyone, by Carl W.
    Battle. Allworth Press, 10 E. 23rd St., New York, NY 10010.
    1996. $18.95. 205 pages.
    (See profile, Chapter 1).

Quicken Family Lawyer 99 Deluxe. Parsons Technology, P.O. Box
   100, Hiawatha, IA 52233-0100. 1998. $39.95. Software.
   (See profile, Chapter 1.)

Incorporation

Do-it-Yourself Kit: Incorporation. E-Z Legal Forms, Inc., 384 S.
   Military Trail, Deerfield Beach, FL 33442. 1998. $21.95. Form
   Kit.
   Includes instructions and forms for incorporating a nonprofit
   corporation.

How to Form a Nonprofit Corporation, by Anthony Mancuso. Nolo
   Press, 950 Parker St., Berkeley, CA 94710. 1997 (4th Ed.).
   $39.95. 368 pages with disk.
   Information on how to form and operate a tax-exempt corporation
   in all 50 states. Includes instructions for obtaining federal 501c(3)
   tax exemption with the IRS.

How to Form Your Own Corporation, by W. Kelsea Eckert, Arthur
   G. Sartorius, III and Mark Warda. Sourcebooks, Inc., P.O. Box
   372, Naperville, IL 60566. 1998 (2nd Ed.). $19.95. 196 pages.
   Step-by-step instructions and the forms you need for incorporating
   in all 50 states and the District of Columbia. Includes state-
   specific information and forms.

*How to Incorporate: A Handbook for Entrepreneurs and Profes-
   sionals,* by Michael R. Diamond and Julie L. Williams. John
   Wiley & Sons, Inc., 605 3rd Ave., New York, NY 10158-0012.
   1996. $19.95. 310 pages.
   Information on how to structure your corporation for maximum
   legal, tax and business advantage. State-specific forms included.

Incorporate Your Business: The National Corporation Kit, by
   Daniel Sitarz. Nova Publishing Co., 1103 W. College St.,
   Carbondale, IL 62901. 1997 (2nd Ed.). $29.95. 253 pages.
   Includes information, forms, checklists and instructions for
   forming a small business corporation.

Incorporation. E-Z Legal Software, 384 S. Military Trail, Deerfield
 Beach, FL 33442. 1998. $29.95. CD-ROM and disks.
 Includes legal forms and documents for incorporating a business
 in any state.

Intellectual Property

*The Copyright Handbook: How to Protect and Use Written
 Words,* by Stephen Fishman. Nolo Press, 950 Parker St., Berke-
 ley, CA 94710. 1998 (4th Ed.). $29.95. 368 pages with disk.
 Step-by-step instructions and the forms necessary to protect all
 kinds of written expression, including works produced on CD-
 ROM or disk, computer databases and electronic mail.

How to Register Your Own Copyright, by Mark Warda.
 Sourcebooks, Inc., P.O. Box 372, Naperville, IL 60566. 1998
 (2nd Ed.). $19.95. 195 pages.
 Information on what a copyright is and the forms you need to
 register your work with the Copyright Office; contains forms for
 registering written, artistic, audiovisual, musical and other works.

How to Register Your Own Trademark, by Mark Warda.
 Sourcebooks, Inc., P.O. Box 372, Naperville, IL 60566. 1997
 (2nd Ed.). $19.95. 180 pages.
 Information on types of trademarks and types of registrations.
 Includes forms and instructions for legally registering your
 trademark.

The Inventor's Notebook, by Fred Grissom & David Pressman.
 Nolo Press, 950 Parker St., Berkeley, CA 94710. 1996 (2nd Ed.).
 $19.95. 240 pages.
 Helps inventors organize important information relating to their
 invention including conceiving, building, testing and legally protecting their invention. Marketing and financing strategies also
 given.

License Your Invention: Take Your Great Idea to Market with a Solid Legal Agreement, by Richard Stim. Nolo Press, 950 Parker St., Berkeley, CA 94710. 1998. $39.95. 500 pages.
Learn how to enter into a good written agreement with manufacturers, marketers or distributors who will handle the details of manufacturing your invention. Sample tear-out agreements and form disk included.

Patent, Copyright and Trademark, by Stephen Elias. Nolo Press, 950 Parker St., Berkeley, CA 94710. 1997 (2nd Ed.). $24.95. 448 pages.
Provides an overview of patent, copyright, trademark and trade-secret law; sample non-disclosure agreements; and patent, copyright and trademark forms.

Patent It Yourself, by David Pressman. Nolo Press, 950 Parker St., Berkeley, CA 94710. 1997 (6th Ed.). $44.95. 480 pages.
Step-by-step information and forms for obtaining a U.S. patent. Also provides an overview of the procedures for getting patent protection and information on marketing your invention.

Software Development: A Legal Guide, by Stephen Fishman. Nolo Press, 950 Parker St., Berkeley, CA 94710. 1998 (2nd Ed.). $44.95. 576 pages /CD ROM.
Step-by-step instructions and forms needed to register a software copyright with the U.S. Copyright Office.

Software Law, Todd F. Bassinger. Sourcebooks, Inc., P.O. Box 372, Naperville, IL 60566. 1997. $29.95. 243 pages.
Explains how to file the proper registration forms to obtain legal protection for your software and explains the different types of protection available.

The Patent Drawing Book: How to Prepare Formal Drawings Required by the U.S. Patent Office, by David Pressman. Nolo Press, 950 Parker St., Berkeley, CA 94710. 1997. $29.95. 256 pages.
A companion to Pressman's "Patent It Yourself," this book shows inventors how to create their own patent drawings that comply with the strict rules of the U.S. Patent Office.

Trademark: Legal Care for Your Business & Product Name, by Kate McGrath & Stephen Elias. Nolo Press, 950 Parker St., Berkeley, CA 94710. 1997 (3rd Ed.). $29.95. 352 pages.
Step-by-step instructions and the forms you need for registering a federal trademark or service mark with the U.S. Patent and Trademark Office.

Property
Every Landlord's Legal Guide, by Marcia Stewart, Ralph Warner and Janet Portman. Nolo Press. 950 Parker St., Berkeley, CA 94710. 1997 (2nd Ed.). $34.95. 496 pages.
(See profile, Chapter 3.)

Every Tenant's Legal Guide, by Janet Portman and Marcia Stewart. Nolo Press. 950 Parker St., Berkeley, CA 94710. 1997 (2nd Ed.). $24.95. 350 pages.
(See profile, Chapter 3.)

The For Sale By Owner Kit, by Robert Irwin. Dearborn Financial Publishing, Inc., 155 N. Wacker Dr., Chicago, IL 60606-1719. 1996 (2nd Ed.). $15.95. 199 pages.
Information on how to sell your property without hiring a broker or lawyer.

How to Buy a Condominium or Townhome, by Irwin E. Leiter. Sourcebooks, Inc., P.O. Box 372, Naperville, IL 60566. 1997. $16.95. 166 pages.
(See profile, Chapter 3.)

How to Negotiate Real Estate Contracts, by Mark Warda.
   Sourcebooks, Inc., P.O. Box 372, Naperville, IL 60566. 1998
   (3rd Ed.). $16.95. 166 pages.
   (See profile, Chapter 3.)

How to Negotiate Real Estate Leases, by Mark Warda.
   Sourcebooks, Inc., P.O. Box 372, Naperville, IL 60566. 1998
   (3rd Ed.). $16.95. 162 pages.
   (See profile, Chapter 3.)

Leases & Rental Agreements, by Marcia Stewart and Ralph
   Warner. Nolo Press, 950 Parker St., Berkeley, CA 94710.
   1996. $18.95. 160 pages.
   (See profile, Chapter 3.)

Small Business
*Business Lawyer: 301 Legal Forms & Agreements for Every
   Business Need.* E-Z Legal Forms, Inc., 384 S. Military Trail,
   Deerfield Beach, FL 33442. 1997. $29.95. Software.
   (See profile, Chapter 7.)

BUSINESS LetterWorks, by Strategic Communications. Round
   Lake Publishing, 31 Bailey Ave., Ridgefield, CT 06877. 1993.
   $79.95. 470 pages.
   (See profile, Chapter 7.)

Corporate Secretary, by Mario D. German. E-Z Legal Forms,
   Inc., 384 S. Military Trail, Deerfield Beach, FL 33442. 1994.
   $24.95. 244 pages.
   Contains more than 170 ready-to-use minutes, resolutions,
   notices and waivers to keep corporate records. Valid in all 50
   states.

Do-It-Yourself Limited Liability Company, E-Z Legal Forms, Inc., 384 S. Military Trail, Deerfield Beach, FL 33442. 1997. $14.95. 130 pages.
Instructions and information on organizing and operating a limited liability company. Includes fill-in-the-blank forms and limited liability company requirements and registration by state.

Form Your Own Limited Liability Company, by Anthony Mancuso. Nolo Press, 950 Parker St., Berkeley, CA 94710. 1998 (2nd Ed.). $34.95. 336 pages.
Provides step-by-step instructions and all the forms you need to set up a limited liability company anywhere in the United States. Includes the latest IRS tax classifications for limited liability companies.

How to Form and Operate a Limited Liability Company, by Gregory C. Damman. Self-Counsel Press, 1704 N. State St., Bellingham, WA 98225. 1998 (2nd Ed.). $16.95. 222 pages.
Explains what a limited liability company is, what types of companies qualify and how to create one. Sample forms and state-by-state directory of information included.

How to Form Your Own Partnership, by Edward A. Haman. Sourcebooks, Inc., P.O. Box 372, Naperville, IL 60566. 1998. $19.95. 183 pages.
Step-by-step instructions and the forms you need to create a legal partnership in all 50 states and Washington, DC.

How to Write a Business Plan, by Mike McKeever. Nolo Press, 950 Parker St., Berkeley, CA 94710. 1997 (4th Ed.). $21.95. 272 pages.
Explains how to write a business plan by making realistic financial projections, developing effective marketing strategies and defining overall business goals. Includes sample business plans and fill-in-the-blank financial forms.

Kiplinger Small Business Attorney. Block Financial Corporation, 4435 Main Street, Kansas City, MO 64111. 1996. $49.95. Software.
(See profile, Chapter 7.)

Legal Guide for Starting & Running a Small Business, Volumes 1 and 2, by Fred S. Steingold. Nolo Press, 950 Parker St., Berkeley, CA 94710. 1997 (1st Ed.). $24.95. 344/340 pages.
A two-volume set with everything a small business owner needs to know about starting and running a business. Volume 2 includes over 75 legal forms and documents and step-by-step instructions for filling the forms out.

Quicken Business Law Partner 3.0. Parsons Technology, P.O. Box 100, Hiawatha, IA 52233-0100. 1998. $29.95. Software.
(See profile, Chapter 7.)

Simplified Small Business Accounting, by Daniel Sitarz. Nova Publishing Co., 1103 W. College St., Carbondale, IL 62901. 1996. $19.95. 254 pages.
Provides a basic understanding of accounting and bookkeeping, and the forms you need to keep clear and accurate business financial records.

Small Business Legal Pro 3.0 (Deluxe). Nolo Press, 950 Parker St., Berkeley, CA 94710. 1997. $79.95. Software.
(See profile, Chapter 7.)

Small Time Operator, by Bernard B. Kamoroff. Bell Springs, P.O. Box 1240, Willits, CA 95490. 1998 (23rd Ed.). $16.95. 180 pages.
Information and step-by-step instruction for starting a small business, including buying envelopes, purchasing insurance, applying for permits and licenses and more.

Smart Business Legal Smarts, by Deborah L. Jacobs. Bloomberg
    Small Business, 100 Business Park Dr., Princeton, NJ 08542.
    1998. $16.95. 210 pages.
    A source guide for business owners. Answers the most com-
    monly asked questions of business professionals.

Standard Legal Forms and Agreements for Small Business, by Steve
    Sanderson. Self-Counsel Press, Inc., 1704 N. State St.,
    Bellingham, WA 98225. 1990. $14.95. 198 pages.
    (See profile, Chapter 7.)

Starting a Limited Liability Company, by Martin M. Shenkman,
    Samuel Weiner and Ivan Taback. John Wiley & Sons, Inc., 605
    3rd Ave., New York, NY 10158-0012. 1996. $19.95. 248 pages.
    Information on what a limited liability company is and what you
    need to do to set up and operate one. Includes checklists, sample
    legal forms and a glossary of terms.

The Complete Book of Business & Legal Forms, Lynne Ann
    Frasier. Sourcebooks, Inc., P.O. Box 372, Naperville, IL 60566.
    1996. $18.95. 268 pages.
    (See profile, Chapter 7.)

The Complete Book of Small Business Legal Forms, by Daniel
    Sitarz. Nova Publishing Co., 1103 W. College St., Carbondale,
    IL 62901. 1997. $29.95. 253 pages.
    (See profile, Chapter 7.)

The Law (in Plain English) for Small Businesses, by Leonard D.
    DuBoff. Allworth Press, 10 E. 23rd St., New York, NY 10010.
    1998 (3rd Ed.). $19.95. 245 pages.
    Covers a variety of issues of interest to business owners including
    business organization, intellectual property issues, licensing,
    advertising and cyberspace law.

The Most Valuable Business Legal Forms You'll Ever Need, by
   James C. Ray. Sourcebooks, Inc., P.O. Box 372, Naperville, IL
   60566. 1996. $19.95. 165 pages.
   (See profile, Chapter 7.)

The Most Valuable Corporate Forms You'll Ever Need, by James
   C. Ray. Sourcebooks, Inc., P.O. Box 372, Naperville, IL 60566.
   1998 (2nd Ed.). $24.95. 249 pages.
   Provides instructions and over 100 forms to help you run your
   corporation legally, efficiently and profitably.

The Partnership Book: How to Write a Partnership Agreement, by
   Denis Clifford and Ralph Warner. Nolo Press, 950 Parker St.,
   Berkeley, CA 94710. 1997 (5th Ed.). $34.95. 304 pages with
   disk.
   Information and the forms you need to create a partnership. Also
   what to do if a partner leaves the business, dies or wants to buy
   you out.

Taxes

The Ernst & Young Tax Saver's Guide, 1999. John Wiley & Sons,
   Inc., 605 3rd Ave., New York, NY 10158-0012. 1999. $12.95. 302
   pages.
   (See profile, Chapter 4.)

J.K. Lasser's Your Income Tax, 1999. Macmillan Publishing Co., 201
   W. 103rd St., Indianapolis, IN 46290. 1999. $14.95. 758 pages.
   (See profile, Chapter 4.)

Kiplinger TaxCut–Multi-State Edition. Block Financial
   Corporation. 4435 Main Street, Kansas City, MO 64111.
   1997. $24.95. Software.
   This Windows and Mac software contains 24 state editions on
   one CD-ROM (only five for Mac though). The software
   enables you to transfer data from your federal return, and
   print your ready-to-file state return.

Quicken Turbo Tax. Intuit, Inc. 2650 E. Elvira Rd., Tucson, AZ 85706. 1998. $34.95. Software.
(See profile, Chapter 4.)

Stand Up to the IRS, by Frederick W. Daily. Nolo Press, 950 Parker St., Berkeley, CA 94710. 1997. $24.95.
Provides all the forms necessary for dealing with the IRS and Tax Court, as well as confidential forms used by the IRS during audits and collection interviews.

Top Tax Saving Ideas for Today's Small Business, by Thomas J. Stemmy. Oasis Press/PSI Research, P.O. Box 3727, Central Point, OR 97502. 1996. $16.95. 317 pages.
A reference guide that explains complex tax laws in plain language. Identifies tax saving areas and arms business people with the information they need to work knowledgably with professional advisors.

ABOUT HALT

HALT–*An Organization of Americans for Legal Reform* is a national, non-profit, non-partisan public-interest group of more than 50,000 members. It is dedicated to helping all Americans handle their legal affairs simply, affordably and equitably. HALT pursues an ambitious education and advocacy program to improve the quality, reduce the cost and increase the accessibility of the civil legal system.

HALT works at both the state and federal levels to:

- Reform "unauthorized practice of law" rules that forbid nonlawyers from handling even routine uncontested matters, limit consumers' options and make legal services unaffordable to many.
- Assure consumer protection against incompetence and fraud by replacing lawyer self-regulation with public control and accountability in the discipline systems for lawyers and judges.
- Develop standardized do-it-yourself forms and simplified procedures for routine legal matters such as wills, uncontested divorces, trusts and simple bankruptcies.
- Promote pro-consumer reforms in small claims, probate and the civil justice system.

To achieve its educational goals, HALT publishes *Citizens Legal Manuals* like this one and an *Everyday Law Series* of brief legal guides to increase consumers' ability to handle their own legal affairs and help them become better-informed users of legal services. Written in easy-to-understand language, these materials explain basic legal principles and procedures, and include step-by-step instructions.

HALT's quarterly publication, *The Legal Reformer,* is the only national periodical of legal reform news and analysis. It informs readers about major legal reform developments and what they can do to help.

HALT's activities are funded through member contributions and foundation support.

JOIN HALT

HALT accomplishes its mission through the generous support of its 50,000 members. We need you!

❑YES!

I want to help reform America's civil justice system. Enclosed are my membership dues of:

❑ $20 (minimum)   ❑ $100
❑ $35   ❑ $250
❑ $50   ❑ $500

Please charge my contribution to:
❑ VISA   ❑ Mastercard   ❑ American Express

Credit Card No._____

Expiration date_____

Signature_____

Name_____

Address_____

City_____ State_____Zip_____

Phone_____ e-mail_____

BENEFITS OF HALT MEMBERSHIP

- A free copy of *Using a Lawyer...And What To Do If Things Go Wrong*.
- *Action Alerts* reporting on legal reform developments in your state.
- HALT's quarterly newsletter, *The Legal Reformer*.
- A voice for your concerns about the lack of accessibility and affordability of America's civil justice system.

1612 K Street, NW, Suite 510
Washington, DC 20006
phone - (202) 887-8255
fax - (202) 887-9699
e-mail halt@halt.org http://www.halt.org